Changing the Message

Changing the Message

Cruelty to Persons Who Are Gay
Is Incompatible
with Christian Teaching

Julie Wood

Grateful Steps
Asheville, North Carolina

Grateful Steps Foundation
30 Ben Lippen School Road #107
Asheville, North Carolina 28806
Copyright © 2020 by Julie Wood
Library of Congress Control Number 2020938823
ISBN 978-1-945714-46-7 Paperback
Printed in the United States of America at Lightning Source
FIRST EDITION
Wood, Julie
Changing the Message:
Cruelty to Persons Who Are Gay Is
Incompatible with Christian Teaching.
Cover illustration by Lacy Wood.
All photos are from the author's personal collection unless otherwise specified.

–The Scripture quotation marked NLT is taken from the *Holy Bible, New Living Translation,* copyright © 1996, 2004, 2007, 2013, 2015 by Tyndale House Foundation. Used by permission of Tyndale House Publishers, Inc., Carol Stream, Illinois 60188. All rights reserved.

–The Scripture quotation marked NIV:THE HOLY BIBLE, NEW INTERNATIONAL VERSION® NIV® Copyright © 1973, 1978, 1984 by International Bible Society®Used by permission. All rights reserved worldwide.

–The Scripture quotation marked RSV: *Revised Standard Version of the Bible,* copyright © 1946, 1952, and 1971 National Council of the Churches of Christ in the United States of America. Used by permission. All rights reserved worldwide.

–The Scripture quotations marked KJV are from *The King James Version* of the Bible, Oxford University Press, 1873. Not under copyright.

–The Scripture quotation marked ESV: *English Standard Version of the Bible* is not under copyright, the copyright having expired.

Music lyrics on page 130: CREEP. Words and Music by THOM YORKE, JONATHAN GREENWOOD, PHILIP SELWAY, COLIN GREENWOOD, EDWARD O'BRIEN, ALBERT HAMMOND and MIKE HAZELWOOD © 1992 WARNER/CHAPPELL MUSIC LTD. and RONDOR MUSIC (LONDON) LTD.All Rights in the U.S. and Canada for WARNER/CHAPPELL MUSIC LTD. Administered by WB MUSIC CORP.
{Incorporates THE AIR THAT I BREATHE by ALBERT HAMMOND and MIKE HAZELWOOD, © 1972, 1973 (Copyrights Renewed) RONDOR MUSIC LTD. (LONDON)}All Rights Reserved. Used By Permission of ALFRED MUSIC

Publisher's Cataloging-In-Publication Data
(Prepared by The Donohue Group, Inc.)
Names: Wood, Julie (Julie H.), 1963- author.
Title: Changing the message : cruelty to persons who are gay is incompatible with Christian teaching / Julie Wood.
Description: First edition. | Asheville, North Carolina : Grateful Steps, [2020]
Identifiers: ISBN 9781945714467 (paperback) | ISBN 9781945714504 (ebook)
Subjects: LCSH: Homosexuality--Religious aspects--Christianity. | Homophobia--Religious aspects--Christianity. | Respect for persons. | Wood, Ben (William Benjamin), 1991-2013. | Wood, Julie (Julie H.), 1963- | Parents of gays--United States. | Gay college students--Suicidal behavior--United States.
Classification: LCC BR115.H6 W66 2020 (print) | LCC BR115.H6 (ebook) | DDC 261.835766--dc23

iv

I dedicate this book:
– to those who needlessly suffer just for being as God beautifully created them.
– to all who have suffered alongside the harmed and have been unable to protect.
– to those who feel they must label and reject another person. I pray seeds of new awareness may sprout and grow.
– to the grief stricken and lost. I pray they may receive hope.
– to all whom I love, those who love me and those who need to know that someone cares . . . even a stranger.

Contents

CONTENTS

PROLOGUE

The day was ordinary. Even though evening was approaching, the sun shone brightly. Bill was mowing the grass in the front yard and was just past a group of three small trees in front of our bay window. The girls and I were doing normal summer evening things. I don't remember exactly, but I may have been preparing dinner. Ben was not with us. He had gone to the church for an extra youth meeting to complete the final planning for a mission trip. It would be only a few days until the youth group would load the church bus and head for the mission site.

Although the group had increasingly become a nest of conflict, confusion and stress, Ben really wanted to see this trip through. He loved helping paint, build porches or whatever else would benefit someone in need. "This is what the church is all about," he told me. He also loved the camaraderie, teamwork and fun. He had committed to the mission trip.

The teachings of the new leader were upsetting and contradictory to anything that Ben had been taught. Our meetings with church leadership had been supportive and understanding, yet we could not see any improvement in the behavior of this charismatic youth leader. We agreed that after the trip, a decision would be made. Should we leave a group that has been so dear or tough it out and try to help open eyes? Ben, Bill and I had each commented, "If we run away and leave, it will not change." Later, I wondered why we thought it was appropriate to step in as the sacrificial lambs. If only we had recognized the need to protect ourselves, our family and especially our dear, brilliant, sensitive, social justice-seeking son.

***

As I walked into the family room about ninety minutes after Ben had left, Ben's car caught my eye through the bay window. It was fast and abrupt as it whipped into our driveway. *Something is wrong! He is home early.* I quickly walked to the front door. As I opened the door, Ben ran up the steps to our front porch. The intensity was palpable. The beautiful green eyes of my 16-year-old child locked directly into mine. Tears filled his lids in a pool that was just about to spill over. His cheeks were flushed, his breathing rapid and his lips . . . oh his lips quivered as he formed words with great effort and despite the contortion of his face on the verge of crying.

"He has yelled at me for an hour!" Ben said. "He made my friends say they were not comfortable with me and that I was going to hell. 'I'm sorry for anything I have done,' I told him. He said that he did not believe me."

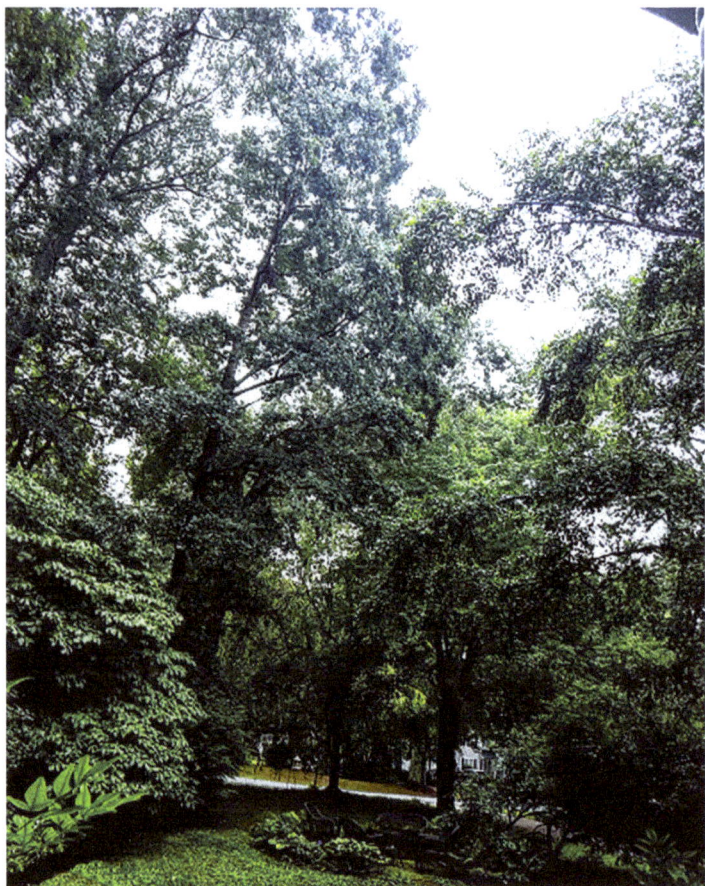

This canopy of trees the author saw during grief and
shock brought a spiritual message.

CHAPTER ONE

THE TREES

I separated myself from the talking, the varying ringtones, what was known being told again and again. For me, briefly, all of the activity blurred into white noise. I became aware of my shattered and empty state but was drawn to look up at the canopy of trees above me. My first very simple and exhausted thought was, *How can the trees still be green when the world has become so very dark and gray?* Bewilderment seemed to take me to an illogical rawness. I felt the darkness of shattered lostness that I had no skills to comprehend, yet in this brief moment, tall and strong trees were sheltering my soul. New, green, spring leaves shimmered with light that was making way through the spaces between the leaves. I was aware that I was—in some spiritual way—being held. I could at least acknowledge that light still existed in the beautiful wisdom of nature.

CHAPTER TWO

THE LAST FEW DAYS

On Saturday, May 4, 2013, I turned 50! In following our typical tradition, Bill, Mom and the girls took me out to eat. Fifty felt so big! It did seem a little odd that I did not hear a word from Ben. I was sure that he was in a flurry because he was ending up his college semester with exams and packing up, and I knew that he would be home in just four days.

When I arrived at work on Monday morning, I found my office filled with balloons; my desk covered with metallic blue, burgundy and gold confetti in shapes of birthday hats and cake and bearing the words Happy Birthday; and my credenza graced with flowers that had arrived from my sister. I worked with such beautiful, kind and fun people!

I knew this was going to be a week so busy that we would need to take the logistics one day at a time. After work on Monday, we hurried home to quickly prepare and have dinner, make sure Lacy dressed for her middle school chorus concert, and let the dogs out. After we finished up, we left for the school, leaving the dirty dishes and pans on the counter. Sophie said that her throat was getting sore.

The next morning there was the usual mad rush to get everyone out the door with lunches in hand, the pets cared for and plans reviewed for another busy night. Our new, young dog, Malachi, was creating particular challenges as he seemed to chew everything. There was a growing disarray in the house. More dirty dishes were left as the mess of the house grew. While herding everyone out the door, my mind was working out the details for the completion of the last of a string of interviews I would be conducting for a manager's position.

After I arrived at the office, I gathered needed items for the interviews, assessed my office and realized that I should clean up from my birthday celebration the day before. I began to brush confetti off my desk, my office chairs and my table, but there were stubborn pieces stuck to the carpet. *Well, I just have to get that up later.* I neatened up my cards and took a moment to enjoy the fresh flowers. Then I entered a day of rushed back-to-back interviews.

Toward the end of the day, I heard from Sophie after she was home from school. Her throat continued to hurt. I called the pediatrician and managed to get a late appointment. After rushing from the office, I picked up Sophie, and we arrived at the doctor's office. The strep throat culture was negative, but the doctor said that she would get more definitive results the next day. We ran home, cooked dinner, put pets out, stacked up more dishes and clothes, dashed past the items that had been chewed up by Malachi, ensured Lacy was dressed as instructed, this time for an orchestra concert—black pants and white blouse—and off we went to the concert. My husband, Bill, and I commented on the extreme demands of the week. We had not even had the opportunity to ready Ben's room as we normally did.

While sitting in the audience, I noticed Sophie sending Ben pictures of Malachi. She texted, "I can't wait for you to meet him tomorrow!"

That night, after everyone went to bed, it was quiet, and I could be alone with my thoughts a bit. I knew I needed to make a decision about which manager to hire. I sat at our dining room table and began to write. I made a grid that graphed out the strengths and experiences of each candidate and how each asset could be used effectively in our team. I was especially struggling between two people. I was up rather late. I felt uneasy, stressed and ungrounded. Life was just so busy and my mind was overworking.

My mommy gut felt no intuitive worries about my Ben. I didn't energetically or emotionally feel any heightened concern for him. I just knew that he would be home the next day, and I could not wait.

Wednesday, May 8, 2013, I had not slept well at all. It was a night of working in my sleep. I was awake early and oddly sat at the kitchen table for a few minutes and thought about the fact that I had just turned 50. I stopped from the crazy business of the present and began listing the things that I would like to accomplish with the remainder of my life and especially this year. I was feeling very inspired from an article that I read about someone who had completely changed her health in her 50s. This is something that I wanted very much. I had many weight loss failures throughout my adult life but thought, *I want to try again.*

It was time for me to get everyone up. *Hurry up,* I told myself. Sophie still felt bad with a sore throat. I thought, *Well, we really don't know for sure that it is not strep.* I shared with my coworkers that Sophie was sick. I told them I would be a little late but that I would just come in for a brief meeting and pack up some of my things to work from home. I looked around and thought, *This house is atrocious, but I can't do anything about it now.* I propped pillows behind Sophie on the sofa, covered her with a cozy blanket, brought her warm tea with lemon and honey and placed the phone on her lap. The TV was playing a movie for her and big Malachi was by her side. While intentions were filled with love and care, oh how many times I have had to wrestle with the guilt of Sophie being alone.

I called my mom, who lived at an assisted living facility, and asked, "Will you call Sophie at least every thirty minutes until I return?"

"Oh yes!" she said. "I always love to help."

Sophie was very proud and excited to stay alone for a short period of time. I told her, "I will be back by one o'clock and will keep my phone right with me." We reviewed safety rules.

Sophie had a little smile as I told her that I would see her in a little bit.

The last day of my old life was underway. I first stopped by the store to pick up birthday cookies for our administrative assistant. At the office, I began to gather items to work from home.

My cell phone rang at 12:20. It was Sophie.

CHAPTER THREE

THE CALL/THE JOLT OF AN UNANTICIPATED NEW LIFE

Sophie said, "Mom, there are two policemen here, and one wants to talk to you."

"Hello."

The responding voice was firm but kind, "Ma'am, this is Officer ____. Ma'am, no one is in trouble. No one has done anything wrong, but I need you to come home right away. How long will it take you?"

"About twenty minutes," I said.

I immediately grabbed my bag and started out my office door where I intercepted some coworkers who looked at me in a questioning way. I said, "There are police at my house. I have to go."

One asked, "Can I go with you?"

"No," I said. "I'm sure everything is okay. It's odd, but it should be fine."

Another worker looked at me as if responding in concern to my expression.

I repeated, "The police are at my house. I have to go home."

***

While driving home, I thought, *Okay, what can it be? Bill?* I called his work. He was in a meeting. Okay, he is fine. I left a message for him to call. *Mom? No, the police wouldn't come.*

I called Sophie. Sophie was afraid. I deliberately kept my voice calm.

She said, "When the two officers came to the door, I didn't know whether to open it." She paused. "I talked to them through the bay window. Staying inside with Malachi, I dialed your number, opened the door just a little, gave them the phone and locked the door back."

I said, "Sophie, you handled this perfectly. I am so very proud of you." I approached stopped traffic. I said, "Honey, the traffic is slow, but I am coming. I am going to stay on the phone with you." I felt that by being on the phone, she was with Malachi and me.

She asked, "Am I in trouble for missing school?"

Chapter Four

THE OFFICERS

The traffic did not slow me down more than five minutes, and I was soon in my neighborhood. I made the left turn into our cul-de-sac and could see two police cars parked just past my house. I pulled in my driveway and parked as the cars pulled in behind me.

I got out of the car and smiled at the officers. "Hello. How are you?"

They spoke gently and smiled slightly. "May we go inside, please?"

We all walked into the home. I scanned the family room. I was mortified! On the floor were chewed papers, plastic, and even a picture frame; covers lay all over the sofa; a dead plant—that I was hoping to put out in the spring to bring back—sat by the window; and several layers of dishes were visible in the kitchen. The house was at its absolute worst! This is what my mind was on. I was so embarrassed and full of shame.

We stood in the middle of the room. I asked Sophie, "Will you go upstairs, honey, while I talk to the officers?"

One of the officers said, "Ma'am, can you show me some identification, please?"

I picked back up my pocketbook, dug through for my wallet, and as my fingers filed through my cards, I noticed that my hands were quivering. I wonder if my body knew before my mind did. I found my license.

The officer had a small notebook and began recording my information as I waited. When he finished, he took a deep breath as the other officer stood solemnly but kindly by. "Do you have a son in Asheville?" he asked.

I nodded. "Yes."

"Ma'am. He is no longer with us."

CHAPTER FIVE

PAIN OVERTIME

"He's been in pain overtime."

These were the first words I heard as my son was lifted out of me.

The pregnancy journey had been a difficult one. Soon after learning that we were expecting, we entered a world that we knew only through text books. Bill transformed from a sharply-dressed husband and a confident, almost cocky leader to one who was barely recognizable. His posture was bent over, his pants drooped and his face was unshaven. He gazed deeply into my eyes with his eyes full of tears that ran down his face in a plea for help. This young man in his late 20s became a sorrowful, tortured, frail soul. Even though each of our college majors were in human services, it was so different when the symptoms fell on our little home. Our world became insecure and frightening. While in the midst of crisis, the incredible being continued to develop in my womb.

Bill was afraid of not being a good father and obsessed about not being worthy of God's love. At first it seemed that he was just working through insecurities. His ability to function, however, declined. His ability to follow conversations, lead meetings or make decisions became impossible. He declined steadily until he landed in a fetal position on the couch with tears streaming down from his bloodshot eyes. Work was out of the question. The quest for help became a part of our daily life for several days.

Finally, an appointment . . . but we had to wait for the day of evaluation. Friends, including our pastor and our families, took shifts so that I could go to the place where we both worked each day. I tried to maintain my job duties, help with his and field questions. He was a nursing home administrator, and I was the social worker. Adrenaline circulated through my body that housed my little growing baby.

At the first appointment with a psychiatrist, Bill was diagnosed with major depression. Help arrived through medication and later counseling. Bill began the journey of returning to us. This was his first episode of depression.

Like an old friend who had been away for a while, Bill came back. There was excitement around the pregnancy. We readied our house and enjoyed baby showers. Bill enthusiastically accepted a position to open a new nursing home in a nearby town. He was doing great! He improved and the pregnancy advanced, yet all was not well. My blood pressure began to rise, migraines were relentless and their duration seemed to never end, and I began to have spotting. I had planned to leave my social work position closer to my due date, but the doctor took me out of work a bit sooner to be placed on bed rest. With each OB visit, I hoped for the best and tried to prepare for the worst. Wonderfully, each visit indicated a healthy baby . . . a boy by sonogram.

Three days before my due date, I went for my routine check. It was exciting to go to the obstetrician because I could hear the baby's heart beat as well as get a glimpse with an ultrasound! The nurse escorted me to a room with a recliner with a machine beside it. She explained that we were going to do a nonstress test. She placed a monitor on my belly and a button in my hand that I was to press each time I felt the baby move. As soon as I felt quivers and bumps, I would press my button. The machine printed a long strip of paper that graphed the movement in comparison to my baby's heartbeat. After a time, the nurse came back into the room, evaluated the paper, tore if off the machine and left the room. I was at ease, thinking about a baby opossum that was in our garage during the night. The poor little thing was so scared as the dogs barked ferociously. I shooed the cute little creature out to freedom at about 3 a.m. My random thoughts were interrupted with a quick-stepped nurse reentering the room. She sweetly said, "You are going to need to go to the hospital right away for a C-section. The baby's heart rate slowed and paused when he moved. He is in distress. It is called bradycardia."

She took me quickly to her office to call Bill. I stayed pretty calm when I was telling him, but my eyes were tearing up and my voice began to crack. Everyone, my family, seemed so far away.

***

It was such a strange feeling, driving myself to the hospital, although only a block away, and riding up the elevator to the maternity floor, having no labor pains and alone. I felt as if I were observing myself. Courtesies on the elevator seemed completely out of place.

When I arrived on the unit, a monitor was immediately placed on my belly. Surprisingly, my baby's heart beat was steady. "Everything appears to be just fine," the nurse explained. As if someone had applied the brakes, everything slowed down to a more casual pace. The clinical team prepared me for surgery, and my family arrived.

***

The nurses wheeled me on a gurney down the hall to the operating room. Bill walked beside me with a gown and mask and hat. After a spinal block, I lay on the table with a blue curtain draped in front of me. A pediatrician arrived to await the at-risk baby for a quick evaluation. Bill was to my right. The anesthetist fanned him furiously!

From my vantage point behind the blue curtain and from later viewing a video, I learned what happened next. As the doctor reached in and wiggled our baby's head from my freshly opened uterus, he carefully held the little head in his right hand as his left hand unlooped the cord from around my baby's neck in two full turns. The doctor said, "He's been in pain overtime. He's passed meconium. I'm glad we got to him."

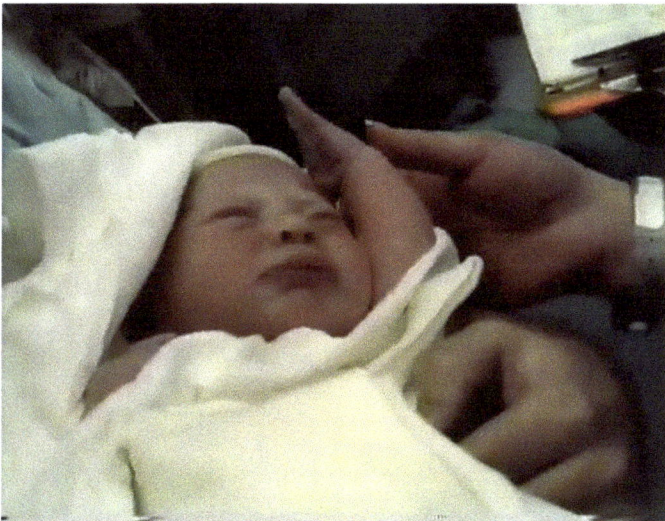

Ben at his birth, 8#7oz.

Lying behind the blue curtain in complete surrender, I could hear a gurgly scream followed by a weak little sound, almost like one shivering. As the pediatrician took my baby boy to the side for further care, the obstetrician said to the pediatrician, "The last one I had like this didn't turn out so good."

Then, as if heaven opened up, I heard a loud, strong, determined cry pierce through the quiet. There was laughter among the medical staff, and the pediatrician commented on the strong lungs!

They later explained their suspicion. When the baby turned a particular way, the cord was pinched, cutting off oxygen, which resulted in life-threatening bradycardia. When he turned back, the cord loosened, and his heart returned to normal. It is frightening to imagine what would have been the outcome if the nonstress test had not occurred at the very moment that my baby boy turned in the direction that produced the crisis. It is frightening to imagine how many times that may have happened during my pregnancy without anyone knowing. A bit of time later, the test may have looked perfectly normal as it did in the maternity ward. I felt very fortunate, protected and blessed.

***

Now, I look back and wonder what it all means. My William Benjamin Wood, born 9/19/1991, my sweet baby, struggled between life and death before he ever took his very first breath.

Sometimes I wonder about the impact of the stress that he must have soaked in while in the womb. While expecting, I eliminated caffeine, took my vitamins, made good food choices and kept my prenatal appointments. But my life during that time was filled with responsibility, fear and the unknown. My little baby.

My world became his experience in utero. But later, Ben's world became my experience.

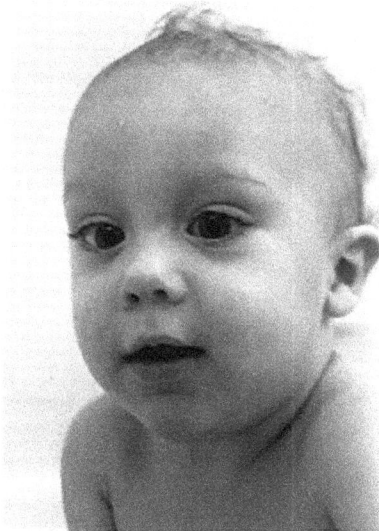

Baby Ben at about 1 year old.
Photo courtesy of Susan Hilliard.

CHAPTER SIX
I HAD TO SAY THE WORDS

I looked down at the floor and saw the scraps that were left from a big, new, young dog's chewing. I started picking them up from the floor. I picked up piece after piece. I was still numbly thinking about the state of the house. Then, I jolted back with a thought of Sophie. I picked up my phone and dialed my dear friend and babysitter, Donna. She had been Ben's babysitter too. Thank God she answered. "I need you, Donna." I said. "Please come." Like a robot, the words were spoken, "Ben is dead. Please come to Sophie. I need you to come to Sophie. She needs you. I need to know that you have her."

Sophie came down and stared into my eyes. "Honey, something very hard has happened," I said. "Ben died." Her little face seemed to freeze. No tears from either of us. We were in a fog.

The officers said, "Ma'am, we need to talk to the coroner right away as well as the school Vice Chancellor." I could hear the officer say with complete authenticity, "We are parents, ma'am. We are so sorry."

"My baby, my sweet, sweet baby." None of this makes sense. We had just been together for spring break.

Ben under a river birch tree.
Photo courtesy of Susan Hilliard.

CHAPTER SEVEN

SPRING BREAK

"Yes, we really do!"

My coworker had asked me, "You all really get so excited when he is coming home, don't you?"

It was Friday and Ben was on his way to Winston-Salem! Bill had vacuumed Ben's room, dusted and changed the sheets in preparation for his arrival. He loved to have it nice for him. Ben would be out the entire next week for spring break.

Yep, his car was in the driveway. I entered the house after a long day of work and soon heard Ben coming up the steps from the basement apartment. That was followed by the familiar sound of the opening door rubbing against the floor. I had meant to get the bottom of the door trimmed a bit, but it had not been a significant priority.

"You are home!"

We hugged. His smile was genuine, as always. We then sat down in the family room. I sat on the sofa, and he sat facing me on a footstool. "How is school going?"

With a shrug, "I don't know. Okay, I guess. Fine." Like in many cases, he did not give a lot of detail.

As we caught up, I did notice that he looked a little nervous. It was the way that he positioned his fingers on his left cheek as he talked. We all receive much non-verbal communication. And especially from those we spend much time with, we learn the language not spoken. At other times I had recognized particular gestures, posture . . . even when one knee bent slightly and turned inward. This was the unconscious message that I understood as nervousness. On this day, I gave it little attention because his smile and words seemed fine.

During that week, Ben was engaged with each one of us. He laughed at Bill and with the girls! He and I went to see a movie. Over the years, we had enjoyed going to movies together. This time we saw *Silver Linings Playbook*. While driving to the theater, I put my hand on his hand as I often briefly did, but he responded by immediately moving his hand. I didn't think a thing about it at the time. Still, his words and conversation seemed fine.

While driving home after the movie, I commented about the story, "I surely don't think much of that father!" The father had been very impatient and condemning in regard to his son's mental health.

Ben could often get "judgey," but not this time. He said, "Well, I guess the character just did the best he could."

We ate at our favorite restaurants. One evening, after enjoying Mediterranean food, we came home to watch a movie after the girls went to bed. It was *Argo*, a very intense movie of the Iranian hostage crisis. Nonetheless, we enjoyed the togetherness.

Firming up plans for Ben's senior year in college was on my spring break agenda! I knew that Ben really hoped not to live on campus again.

Ben during college junior year at age 21.
Photo courtesy of Susan Hilliard.

"Ben, I really need to know. Will you be living on campus or not? It effects the money and the plans we need to make."

He looked at me and confidently said, "I know. I will not be living in the dorm next year." Reliving the words in my mind, now knowing what he knew, I question why I did not see the oddity in the way he said that.

One spring break day, Ben came to volunteer at my work at my request. I had suggested, "Volunteering at a nonprofit is good for a resume." All of my work friends enjoyed seeing him. I was so proud. I loved showing him off!

One of the highlights of the week was Sushi Night! The favorite family activity began when Ben was about 17 years old. He decided it would be good to learn to make vegan sushi. He wanted to honor the heritage of his sister Lacy, adopted from China, and also wanted more food options that were vegan.

Ben's desire to not eat animal products began at an early age. When he was 7, he came to me with tears in his eyes and exclaimed, "Mom, I don't want to eat animals. They are God's creatures. How can we eat them?" I assured Ben that if this is important to him, we would work out a healthy diet for him. We would support him. He never once ate meat again. Later, grieving the cruelty of factory farming, he became vegan at 16. Even though he was very passionate about this decision, he did not shame others about feeling differently. He thought others should make their own decisions about what was right or wrong for them.

He researched and watched "how to make sushi" YouTube videos. Ben and I had a great time shopping for the supplies at the Asian grocery store. We bought sushi matts and pretty little dishes for the condiments and all the ingredients we needed. He and I watched the video while we practiced, step by step, until we got it right. From then on, Sushi Night became a family tradition. Bill cooked on the griddle while Ben and I, with sometimes my mom and/or the girls, patted out the rice over the Nori. Ben was especially good with the fancy ones! Every time Ben was home from college, we looked forward to our Sushi Night activities! We had a particular platter that we used to carefully place the sushi in rows. Often, we sprinkled black sesame seeds on the ones that had rice on the outside.

Bill described the Friday of spring break as a Norman Rockwell type scene. He said it was all just so perfect when he walked in from work. I had taken the day off and so had an early jump on the evening plans. Jabbering away and laughing, the girls were at the dining room table, playing games with a few friends, and Ben and I were talking and laughing at the kitchen table where we were making the sushi. Bill flipped on the TV to watch his favorite team and began chopping the vegetables to grill with a frequent interjection into Ben's and my conversation. It did seem perfect! After the feast, Ben stayed with us in the family room to watch the rest of the ballgame. This was very unusual because Ben had no interest in ball games. But he stayed and was interactive with questions, comments and laughter with his dad.

***

The day had come for Ben to go back to school. I had gone to see my mom but did not expect to be long. I was away longer than expected though. When I got back, Ben had already left on the two-and-a-half-hour drive back to school. It had been such a beautiful week! We felt good to have had so much shared joy.

Chapter Eight

THE MEDICAL EXAMINER

The phone of one of the officers rang. It was the medical examiner. The officer handed me the phone. Like the officers, the medical examiner had a kind voice. He said, "Ma'am, this is the hardest part of my job. I am so sorry for your loss. I need to ask questions, please. Did your son have mental health problems?"

"No, sir."

"Did he have a history of cutting?"

"What? No!" *My God, what has happened?*

"Ma'am, he had some cuts; there was some cough syrup, alcohol and an unlabeled empty pill bottle in the room. He must have died early this morning. Ma'am, I know that this is so much information to take in. I am a parent, ma'am. I imagine my own children every time I go out to these scenes. I am just so sorry. We will need to talk again. It is required that his body be autopsied."

At that moment, there was no mention or thought of his strong support of organ donation. I have grieved that his healthy 21-year-old body was not able to save others. That would have mattered to him.

This call was soon followed by the Vice Chancellor of the college. I felt his authentic care and sadness. He said, "The Resident Assistant was completing the end-of-year room checks because each student was required to be out of the dorms. Ben's door was locked. He opened it and found Ben's body in a fetal position on the floor.

"Oh, my God," I said. "That poor boy, the Resident Assistant. I am so sorry that he had this experience."

"The campus police have Ben's phone and computer," the Vice Chancellor said, "but there does not seem to be any significant information. There is only a text from a friend asking why his Facebook was taken down. That was at 2:30 in the morning. There is no note. I will check back with you. I am so sorry. There is no rush to get his belongings, but when you are ready, I will help you."

***

I was still going through the motions. "I'm glad it wasn't a hate crime," I murmured to one of the officers. "I have been afraid that he would be a victim of more hate."

The second officer asked, "Who can we call, ma'am?" It was about then that my phone rang. The caller ID said: BILL. I had nothing . . . no word, no ability. The second officer stepped into this horrific role for me. He had to speak the unspeakable and tell Bill, "There has been a tragedy in Asheville . . ."

Chapter Nine

CONNECTING THE DOTS

As a baby and young child, Ben was the focus of mine and Bill's world, and for a while, he was the only young grandchild, nephew and cousin. He brought so much joy and life into our families.

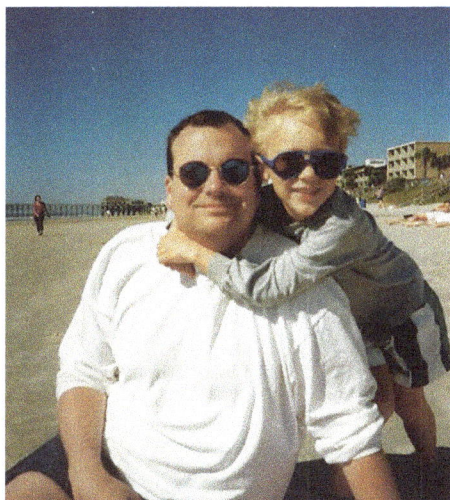

Bill and Ben at the beach.

Ben was treasured. I was able to stay at home until he was 9 months old. I loved his smile and the way he lit up when I entered the room. I enjoyed the giggles when we played simple baby games. I felt so much gratitude to have this baby in my life. He was very bright, inquisitive and was right on target developmentally. Yet, as he grew to a toddler his speech was very difficult to understand and at times impossible. Ben was a small boy with much to say and was relentless in trying to make himself understood. The difficulty communicating was frustrating for him and heartbreaking for me. It was almost as if he was trying to form sounds while having his mouth full of marbles. His little mouth just could not create the sounds that he could hear from the mouths of others.

One night, when Ben was around 3, I tucked him in his little toddler bed after following our bedtime routine. As he slept, Bill and I watched TV until I heard Ben scream. I ran to his room to find him sitting up with tears streaming, horrified from a nightmare. His voice was fast and high pitched as he tried to tell me what had frightened him so. It was evident that he was in that place of not yet figuring out whether the dream was real or not. He spewed it all out. I hung on every syllable. I understood nothing. He tried a second and third time. This was one of the helpless and heartbreaking memories I have. In frustration, he gave up, laid back down, curled up on his side and sobbed as only one could who had no choice but to hold his feelings . . . privately.

More than anything, I wanted to understand and comfort. I tried everything I knew to validate his feelings, easing what I thought to be happening, yet I could not fully understand. Even though his experience was his alone, I tried to soothe my helplessness with knowing that Ben had to feel my love and desire to understand. I patted and rubbed his back. He drifted back to the world of sleep.

Soon after that, I sought out speech therapy. A beautifully kind and loving therapist began the process of building the muscles that are required to make the various sounds of speech. Rs and Ss were the last to develop and remained a very slight inconvenience. Ben fought for and claimed his speech, and Ben had much to say . . . Ben was understood.

Ben absolutely loved his stuffed animals. His all-time favorite, a small beanie-baby hound dog given to him by my brother, slept with him every night . . . Squishy Puppy. He created many stories, roles and relationships involving his stuffed animals. Being an only child, his stuffed animals seemed to be his playmates. He was animated with his stories, danced and laughed with pure joy. There was much excitement any time his twin cousins came to visit. He was always thrilled to have more actors to "put on a show." Looking back, I can see that he came into this life with a love and gift for creativity.

Ben attended our church preschool from 2 to 5. When he was 4, the teachers completed a school readiness assessment. I was a little surprised when the director asked if she could meet with me. She explained, "Ben's little hands are weak, and his coordination and balance are not quite where many the same age might be." She added, "He is not able to grip the crayons or the scissors with control. Sometimes there is a mild type of cerebral palsy." She said, "I suggest further evaluation."

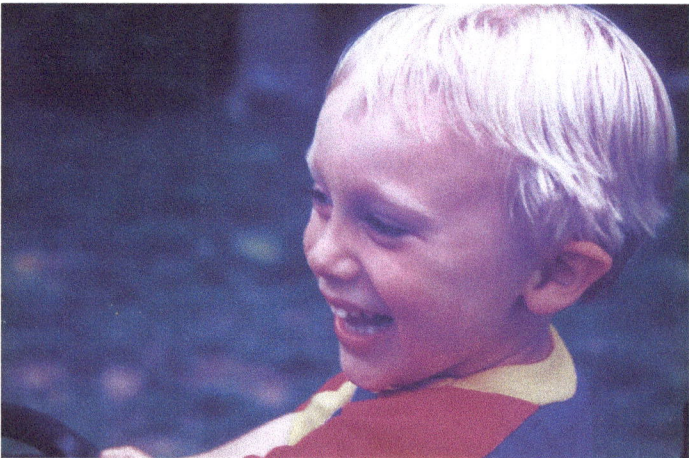

Ben, filled with joy.
Photo courtesy of Susan Hilliard.

Additional testing from a neurologist unhelpfully diagnosed Ben as clumsy. He continued work with the speech therapist at the elementary school. Occupational therapy was added at a local clinic. He worked on balance, sensory integration, building strength in his hands and handwriting. Ben loved kindergarten and delighted in the stories of the "letter people," a typical kindergarten activity to teach the alphabet. By first grade, his difficulty writing became increasingly evident. It could take an hour to write just a handful of words. It was truly painstaking and brought him so much frustration and tears. The school speech therapist and first-grade teacher recommended a School Occupational Therapy Evaluation. From there, it was recommended that he use what was then called an Alpha Smart. He would work on writing in therapy but the Alpha Smart would help him keep up with the other children in completing writing assignments as he typed on an easier keyboard. From then on, Ben used electronics. The first-grade teacher made the accommodation natural. His second-grade teacher had a more authoritative approach and little patience. Ben was very unhappy that year and began to have toileting accidents. I met with the teacher who asked, not in a way of compassion but in a tone of irritation, "What is wrong with him?"

We all knew that there was physical disability, yet his only diagnosis at that time was "clumsy with speech delay." Kids laughed at his speech, although it was still improving, and they sometimes did not care to listen just a little more carefully. His differences were very hard for some to understand. In third grade, his best friend, a very trim, spunky little girl, was said to have held her fist up at some boys in defense of Ben. In the usual uncomfortable playtime scenes, considering that Ben was one who could not kick or catch a ball, the painful choosing up of kickball sides occurred. The competitive boys' captain blurted out to the other team, "You can have two, if you will just take Ben!" The little girl was ready to belt the boy!

By fourth grade, Ben had his own laptop. The technology was an effective way to level the educational playing field for Ben. It had its price though. The technology required a power source. Ben was often positioned by a power source so that his computer could be plugged in. Although intentions were good and appropriate, there is no denying that this created an environmental and symbolic separation from the other students.

**

One time, I watched from the car where I hoped not to be discovered. Several fourth-grade classes were on the playground. The teachers stood on one end where they socialized while they watched over the kids. Boys were playing kickball, and many of the girls were climbing on monkey bars. It was like a beehive of activity. Standing on the side and away from the teachers stood my son. He had on a poofy winter coat and was chewing on his shirt collar. He was so alone and looked as if he wanted to shrink and disappear. This playground was designed for binary activities of well-coordinated children. Those who did not fit into the assigned gender role options and/or did not feel comfort in the available physical activities, had no place to plug in. Rejection and shame appeared woven into the very social structure of recess.

In fifth grade, Ben mentioned on several occasions that he could not jump rope. He said, "I keep trying, and I want to jump rope, but I just can't seem to make my body do it! The gym teacher thinks that I am not trying."

I explained that everyone has different skills.

Later, a teacher's assistant told me, "The gym teacher is really hard on Ben and thinks that he is just lazy. I talked to her but you need to follow up."

Lazy!—he probably put more effort into it and pressure on himself to jump that rope than anyone in the class.

One day, while Ben and I were riding along in our van, Ben solemnly turned toward me and asked, "Mom, what happened to me? Why am I the way I am?"

Ugh, gut punch and panic about how to respond. People-imposed inferiority made Ben feel like damaged goods. I told him that everyone has strengths and weaknesses and that we are all exactly the way God wants us to be, special and unique by design. We were never meant to be the same. I reminded him of the cord being around his neck and his prenatal distress. I said, "Honey, having less oxygen probably affected some coordination and strength, but so what? You are kind and so skilled in so many other ways. You are a perfect Ben."

Ben and lost deer at North Park, Pennsylvania.
Photo courtesy of Susan Hilliard.

Cookie cutters—why in the world does society do everything in its collective power to force people into a particular way of being like each other? And when individuals do not fit into the cookie-cutter mold, why do some others think the individual is wrong or less than. Eye color, hair texture, skin color, place of birth, intelligence, sexual orientation all just beautifully are . . . a part of the intended design. When judgment enters in based on God-given characteristics, we as a people go down a long and dark path of pain and suffering.

***

I work with people who have some sort of intellectual, developmental and/or physical uniqueness. The tendency is to focus on the perceived diagnosis or equipment, such as a wheelchair. While these are things that are important to understand, something magical happens when we can see the soul, the person. I learned some years ago that individuals with lower IQs often have a wisdom that people within typical ranges of intelligence may not ever grow to.

This awareness became real to me about twenty years ago when I met an older individual with whom I worked. His body was mangled with physical differences to include club feet, scoliosis, kyphosis, muscle spasticity and the inability to speak. Intellectually he was evaluated to function at about a 9-month-old level. This dear man routinely greeted me in the mornings by rolling his wheel chair down the hall to meet me with a large, toothless smile. He would then just BE with ME. There were no expectations, judgments or complaints. He simply loved and shared in this experience of life. He had no worry about his needs being met although he was 100% dependent on the care of others. I looked at him often and thought, *How wise is he! How many of us struggle with trust, accepting and just loving? What if we could all accept ourselves, our experiences and those of others, our own and others' vulnerabilities, and just be with and love in such a gentle way.* Ego and pride were not his struggles. Connection and love have been his gifts. He is one of my many teachers.

Chapter Ten

MIDDLE SCHOOL

When Ben got to middle school, the teachers were briefed about his strengths and weaknesses, and, once more, the accommodations needed. One of Ben's teachers, who turned out to be very dear to him, was intimidated at first by the laptop and was horrified that it might be in some way broken. Her nervousness and discomfort were soaked right up by my empathic son. But, overall, sixth grade went very well.

Seventh grade brought different challenges.

While we sat on the front porch steps, Ben said, "Mom, some of the kids are being mean to a kid who is gay."

I reassured him. "Make sure to be his friend, Ben, and tell him that everyone is to be who God made him to be. If it gets bad, talk to the teacher, and if it doesn't improve, let me know if I can help. Let that kid know that the others are wrong!"

Later in the same school year, I noticed that Ben was not drinking anything in the mornings. I learned that he was avoiding the need to go to the bathroom. He was afraid. He was the kid being picked on for being gay, but he was not ready to fully speak the words. Whenever I asked him if he were gay, he just responded, "I don't know." I always had a strong feeling that he should be allowed to tell me in his own time. Ben's self-esteem and sense of belonging had already been compromised before his gender preference was labeled and judged.

Mid-year of seventh grade, we took Ben out of public school and took him to a small-classroom private school. The teachers were very person-centered and loving. But then there was . . . Chapel Time.

"Mom, the chapel teacher said not even to be friends with gay people. I don't understand."

The chapel teacher! My God . . . all Bill and I could think was, *Is there no safe place for our son?* I met with the principal in vain. I expressed my concerns, but he was not willing to make any changes. I tried to help Ben sort through the many condemning messages.

During middle school, Ben had a growing sense of belonging and joy in the church where we were active. He and his friends had a blast in the youth group. This was a time of healing and strength-building. He began to reclaim his value and develop leadership abilities. A cocoon of joy, inspiration, honor and love, the church was a soft and reassuring place to grow. Safe.

I really believed that rejection and belittlement were a part of his past. I said more than once, "He has found himself. He has soared above all the rejection. His experiences have been used to develop wisdom and compassion."

Ben's youth leaders, Doug and wife Beverly, gave the gift of treating Ben as an individual while at the same time treating him just like everyone else. One act of kindness that communicated so much was their devotion to making sure that whatever the active youth group did, there was always a vegetarian food option for Ben. Beautiful. *Isn't it just amazing how acts of kindness can send a force of healing energy into another? Wow, our ripples into the world are very real!*

In addition, Ben was finally given at Wake Forest Baptist Hospital the diagnosis of Diaplegic Cerebral Palsy. I made the appointment after noticing it was so difficult for him to quickly get up from the floor, and he had a lot of foot pain. There were now words to use and documentation in hand. He had appeared to be without a disability, so unreasonable expectations were placed on him at times throughout his life. "His hamstrings are very tight," the neurologist commented, "and he just doesn't have a lot of muscle tone in his hands." We were relieved that there was finally a name we could give.

He used a keyboard proficiently, played the piano and later drove a car without difficulty. We are all a unique mixture of what comes easy and what comes hard, what we like and what we don't. Biology and experience. Human.

Ben, Lacy, Sophie, Easter 2006.
Photo courtesy of Susan Hilliard.

Chapter Eleven

WHEN BILL LEFT

After noticing the caller ID, I had handed the phone to the second officer. He walked away from me and stood by our bay window. I could not focus in on the words. The work friends who had checked on me at the office came through the door. They intuitively knew that I was in crisis. They, like angels, started cleaning my house. More friends arrived, and they started cleaning. I was broken, ashamed and grateful. Donna arrived for Sophie, and one of the friends started making phone calls for me.

As friends and my pastor arrived, we moved out to the front yard where there was a bench away from the messy house. Yes, the state of the house was too often pressing on my mind. Bill's car pulled into the driveway. It was driven by his very close friend and coworker, with another dear friend following in another car. The two sweet ladies went to the passenger's seat to assist their supervisor, the Administrator. I walked over and made the words come out . . . , "Ben died. He killed himself."

With each lady holding an elbow, Bill was walked to the bench where he stayed for what seemed like days. He looked up briefly, looked into my eyes—non-verbally pleading, "Help Me"—and then seemed to let go. He fell far into a bottomless darkness that took him away from us.

***

As I stood in the front yard, my thoughts were interrupted when my focus shifted to a car slowing and pulling into our driveway. *Oh, God, it's Lacy. She has been at gymnastics practice.* My friend making calls for me had arranged for another mother to bring her home. Lacy peered out of the backseat car window and saw all the people and the police. As I approached the car, the backseat door slowly opened. My daughter stepped out in silence while peering into my eyes.

"Lacy, something very hard has happened. Ben died, honey. Ben has died."

She blankly stared, as though unable to grasp the reality, scanned the scene and with no tears numbly walked into the house.

***

Over the next days, neighbors and family walked with Bill in the neighborhood. He shuffled, and if no one was around, he started out walking in the road with no awareness of safety. More than one neighbor picked him up and brought him home. On one occasion, he had left the neighborhood and was found on a busy street. We began to assign people to be with him. He could not eat.

We mixed protein shakes and fed them to him by placing a finger over one end of a straw, placing the straw in the shake to get a manageable mouthful, and dropping the liquid into his mouth. His tongue moved uncontrollably, which is something that I had never seen happen. He was in a semi-catatonic state. His nephew took him to the psychiatrist, but medication changes did not seem to make any difference over the next few weeks. He had been on maintenance medications for depression and anxiety as needed. Previous episodes of depression lasted about two weeks to two months. Although he had experienced four or five episodes of depression, there had not been any episodes in thirteen years.

Malachi, the dog, faithfully checked on each of us and seemed to know just who he should be with. He stayed by Bill's side for hours and hours for days upon days. Malachi was about one year old when we found him. He had been starved, beaten—still cowers when a broom or rake is picked up—and shot; yet amazingly he loved and trusted. We got him just before Ben died. I know that he has been part of our being cared for. He is an angel dog.

Several weeks later, I sat beside Bill with a very sweet, young psychiatry resident. I looked down. The doctor had on the same slip-on, checkerboard, tennis shoes that Ben often wore, and he sat casually with one leg bent under him much like Ben often did. I think that the resemblance added to our comfort while he used his expertise to glue our shattered pieces together the best he could. He was authentic, and at times I could see the hint of a tear about to spill over. Compassion in itself adds healing. After multiple visits with little improvement, we feared hope was fading. The doctor gently and hesitantly explained to me, "Sometimes when trauma occurs, people sort of 'short circuit.' We hope that with time he can improve, but he may not."

CHAPTER TWELVE

THE PATH TO LACY AND SOPHIE

In 1999, Bill, Ben—at age 8—and I vacationed at the beach with our friends Dave, Pam and their daughter, Sara. Sara was adopted from China and was the light of their world. Pam and I had been chatting before the vacation about their desire to adopt a second child. I had wanted another child ever since Ben was a baby, but Bill had felt that our family was complete. One evening after dinner, the adults lingered to talk at the table while Ben and Sara played on the floor of the family room. Ben loved helping look after Sara.

The conversation turned to shared thoughts of adopting, as planned by Pam and me. I said, "How wonderful it would be if both our families adopted, and we could travel together."

Bill, surprisingly, went along with the hypothetical plan until it did not feel hypothetical anymore. I knew I had been sorta draggin' him along, but I felt he was on board.

I could not sleep that night. I was full of joy. I had dreamed and imagined another child so many years but had decided that when I turn 35, I must let go of the dream. Several years prior, I imagined placing all my images, thoughts and dreams of another child onto a blanket, bundling it all together and handing it to God. I did not want to be an older mother. But lying in that bed, I concluded, *It is all working out the way it is supposed to. I know that another child needs what we can give. It felt as if life was falling into place.* As soon as we returned home, applications were obtained to begin step one of the adoption process.

Within days Bill began to share that he did not want to have another child. I was crushed, really crushed, but I accepted that he was being honest and speaking his truth. He loved being a father and had much love to give. I felt sure that his anxiety was a part of this position. I just had to accept. We don't always get what we want.

The time arrived. Dave and Pam received a match to their second daughter and travel plans were underway. They struggled with the idea of both parents being away from Sarah for two weeks. I received a call from Pam asking if I would travel to China with her as her support person. Bill and

Ben were nearby. Bill said, "I think that we'll be fine, won't we Ben?"

I agreed to go and felt really honored. What a privilege! Yet a little voice inside me said, *And you don't get to bring your baby home.* I concluded, *Be a good friend; you can do this and will be amazed at the experience.*

The trip was spectacular. I got to know all the little families in the travel group. Hopes, dreams, plans, insecurities and fears were shared. Some were confident parents and some were anxious first-time parents. But all were very excited and full of anticipation.

Finally, the big day. We were in a room in the hotel in Hefei, China. There was a knock at the door with an ecstatic voice saying, "They are here! The babies are here! Come look!"

All the families ran to an upper level balcony to watch as vans and cars pulled through an underpass. Orphanage personnel stepped out one by one, each with a thickly clothed little bundle. There were guesses as to which baby matched which couple's picture. I soaked in watching these little ones enter their family. I was, however, very upset that I had the zoom all of the way in when it was time to video Maggie being placed in Pam's arms. Therefore, the moment was not captured. Many pictures followed and emails were sent to Dave each day. It was a spiritual experience. Each child's personality seemed to fit right in with the parents.

Chapter Thirteen

A LIFE-CHANGING TOUR

While my role on this journey was as a support person and not an adoptive parent, I was given the gift of stepping stones that directed changes in my life. I am grateful that I recognized them as important. One stone appeared when the travel group visited an orphanage. It was a larger and more progressive site than many. It was a high rise with a square-shaped, open-air courtyard in the middle.

We were completely overwhelmed with the number of little faces peering at us. On one floor, there was a sea of babies sitting in walkers. There were so many that walkers had to be pushed back to open the gate at the top of the steps and pass through. Only minutes into the tour, I noticed a couple huddled away from the others, holding each other and their child with tears streaming for so many left behind. It was so painful to see these little souls group-living. Somewhere in the midst of the sea of babies, I could see across the courtyard to a line of toddlers standing along the hallway. They were watching us too. We continued to file past newborns soundly sleeping two to a bed. As we made our way around the square, we intercepted the line of toddlers. I focused in on a little girl with a puzzled expression. She had a cleft lip. I didn't go to her or interact with her in any way, but I felt somehow drawn to her and her struggle. Her face was beautiful, but I felt concern for her.

The ride back to the hotel was silent other than baby noises and a sniffle here and there. I sat on the bus thinking of the little girl with the cleft lip. What if I can help her? I asked our guide if he could find out her name. I put my finger in front of my lips in an attempt to communicate that the child had a cleft lip. I described the floor where we saw her. Although he spoke English, it did take a deliberate approach to communicate. That night he came to me with her name, Xia. She was 17 months old. This encounter began another leg of the journey that was absolutely life-changing. This little girl became a bridge to our expanded family.

The next day, word spread through the travel group that I had asked for the name of this child. Several members shared pictures of her that they had taken.

It was an experience of a lifetime. I loved watching the babies—who had been among many children whose needs were met in shifts by caring staff but stretched-thin workers—transform to beloved children who had been sought after and waited for. Hearts were pulled and empty spaces were filled with love. This process had God's signature written all over it.

After the long journey home, we were greeted at the airport by a welcome home party. Bill and Ben were there. Ben held a WELCOME HOME sign and beamed with joy as he ran to me when I exited the tarmac. Oh, that little boy.

When I got home, I could just tell that something was off with Bill. Over the next few days, others seemed to let bits of information out. While away, Bill had not been himself, and on Christmas day I learned that life had taken a turn.

This was a hard life chapter. Bill had entered an episode that ended in severe depression. It was the last one until thirteen years later when Ben died.

***

I remembered a man whom I saw in China. This man had demonstrated for me the amazing strength of the human spirit. He became a guide for me. I believe that there are times when we are given tools or opportunities that will give us what we need for future events. There are many instances in which we get exactly what we need.

Pam and Maggie were in the Hefei hotel restaurant finishing lunch. I had some time alone in the hotel room. I stood and looked out the large window. Everyday life unfolded in front of me as if I were watching a documentary. The hotel was beside a busy road and on a steep hill. There were beeping, tiny, blue trucks that looked to me like toys, and red taxis, all abruptly stopping and going. Many horns were blaring. To the right was a lane for everyone and everything else. People were traveling on this narrow lane up the hill by foot, on bicycles, motor bikes—with sometimes entire families balancing onboard. Some were pulling large wagons and some were pushing large loads. In the midst of the hustle and bustle of this average day, I witnessed another scene that I knew to be important. There was a man traveling the narrow path. He was simply living an ordinary day, passing by this hotel window at the very moment that I watched out. This window into the life of this human being has served as a source of wonder and strength for me during some of my most difficult times.

This special soul pushed his load with both arms, hands gripping a metal bar, body bent forward on a cart that was piled so high that he would be able to see only the slats of wood in front of his face, yet he didn't see, because his head was down as he used his strength to push. In this street, congested and bursting with movement, this human blindly powered his load, probably to provide a meager income. Although this was not an unusual site for this street, it was very unusual for me. I watched and wondered, *Does he push this cart every day? Does he wake up each morning and face this task, this challenge, every day? Before going to sleep each night, does he think about what lies ahead in his next day?*

The hill, the piled-high cart, the inability to see ahead was not all! His right leg was twisted in a unique way and bent back behind his left leg. This man had only one leg and foot to use. Laboring up the hill was done one hop at a time.

What was that force that moved that piled-high cart? Where does one find such strength and perseverance? He had tapped into something that I had not. Life had not required it of me.

I have used him as an example, an analogy, many times. While my life unfolded, as with all who walk this earth, I learned later that, like the man in China, I too had tapped into the strength that I did not know was available to me. This image was gifted to me as he demonstrated the magnificent human spirit. I am grateful for this lesson. His example has held and sustained me at times over the last years.

I pray that his circumstances do not define him. I pray that he has joy and fulfillment in each day.

I pray that love surrounds him and his needs are met. He does not know me, but his ripple had a great impact on me. He does not know that I am a part of him and he is a part of me.

***

I found myself struggling between strength and great helplessness. I decided to reach out to the orphanage director in Hefei to see if I could learn more about the child with the cleft lip. I realized while amid the current struggles, there was no way to pursue adoption. I reasoned, *What I can do is help her.* I reached out to Operation Smile and in coordination with the orphanage director, a referral was made. This was all very empowering for me at a time when I needed to feel strength and control. Once Xia was on the list for surgery, barriers presented themselves. She lived on the eastern side of China while the surgery site was in central China. There was a train to get her to the site, but no one to accompany her. After efforts, it just did not seem possible.

Although discouraged, while at a planning meeting for a Walk to Emmaus—a spiritual, nondenominational retreat where I would be one of the speakers—I felt inspired to try to help Xia one more time. When searching for additional contacts and supports in Hefei, I found an article by a professor in Chicago who had written about her experience growing up in a male-preferred society of Hefei, China, and the shame that came upon women for not bearing a son. I decided to email her. I explained that I read her article and that I had recently been to China as a support for a friend who was adopting. I wrote, "There is a little girl who has captured my heart and whom I would like to help." I explained the barriers to her surgery. Much to my surprise, this dear professor reached back to me. She explained that her sister is a reporter in China and that Smile Train, another organization that provides surgery for cleft lip/palate, is scheduled to come to Hefei. Amazingly the sister, along with the orphanage director, was able to get Xia scheduled for surgery. I was able to send a gift that would help support staff from the orphanage who would be providing support at the surgery site.

I found helping Xia to be healing and joyful during a time that I felt very helpless. One morning I awoke and had a clear memory of a dream. I could see a little Asian girl sitting in a high chair pulled up to our kitchen table. She was wearing red. Her hair is what I noticed most but no other details. While in my dream looking at her, I felt a move in my abdomen. In my dream, I thought, *Could I be pregnant?*

Later the Chicago professor was visited in Chicago by a professor from the University in Hefei. The story of my determination to help Xia was shared. The professor from Hefei, upon his return to China, began to visit Xia regularly and sent me reports and pictures. She was doing wonderfully. Later, my professor friend from Chicago went to Hefei China to visit her family. She was able to take Xia to her family's home for a weekend visit. She took videos and sent them to me. This entire experience was incredible. I got to be a part of an experience connected by many acts of kindness.

It was about a year later, when our home was stable, Bill and I were well and Ben was wonderful . . . it happened. We decided to try to adopt Xia. Even though most agencies across the nation said no to pursuing a particular child, we found one in Colorado that agreed to try, yet gave no guarantees. We began to ready our lives for a preschooler.

There is a tremendous amount of paperwork when pursuing adoption, but I found the process much fun! We completed our dossier. One day while I was at work, I received an email from the adoption agency, letting me know there was some paperwork that we had not completed. One particular form had a list of about twenty specified medical conditions, such as a heart defect, cerebral palsy, extra or missing digits, cleft palate. The form prompted me to check yes or no to indicate if we would accept a referral of a child with one of these conditions. I did not know it, but this form was another stepping stone.

I felt confident that we were getting Xia, so I went through the form, during the extreme business of a typical human services provider day, and checked yes to most every item. It was returned without much thought. The process moved fast for us as Xia was considered special needs due to medical follow-up needs.

Then, as life sometimes brings surprises, my doctor diagnosed that I was six weeks pregnant. Wow! While a little shocked at first, this was a moment that I had dreamed of for years.

I will never forget where Bill and I stood when we told Ben. We were at a Putt-Putt place at the Cherry Grove Beach. We stood by a pond on the course and announced, "Ben, we have some exciting news for you. Not only are we adopting a baby, but we are going to have one too!"

His eyes brightened, his hands came together, and he happily asked, "Really?" He did a little happy dance. After that it was announced to the full family.

Soon it was time for the official match. On a Friday and with much excitement, our adoption agency representative called. She said, "All looks positive that you will be officially matched to Xia on Monday. Your application folder is on the match desk."

We were all very excited! This was the news that we had been waiting for.

On Monday, the phone rang and the caller ID indicated it was the adoption agency. Bill, Mom and Ben all came for the news. The news was not what we had expected.

"We are very sorry. Another family submitted a request for Xia. While your application packet arrived at the desk first, the other family's application had been dated earlier. I am so sorry."

Family and friends gathered as if a death had occurred. I sat on the couch and sobbed, "I don't understand." I was shown so much love. I had cared for this child in my heart for some time and told God, "I have to know now that she will be okay. I can release her if I can just be assured."

That very night, I went to the computer, entered a comment to the Waiting Children from China yahoo group and explained what had happened. I said, "Please, if anyone is waiting for your match to this child—I included her name—reach out to me. I have so much to share with you . . . pictures, a video, medical information. Please let me know she will be okay."

I am still in shock that this happened, but an adoptive mother answered me. She explained that when she traveled to China a year after I had been to China and saw the child, she and her husband became friends with another adopting couple while she was there to adopt their own child. The friend couple's adopted child was best friends with Xia. They had requested to adopt her. *Isn't it amazing that I had a good idea which family she would be placed in even before the parents had yet to be notified of the match?*

While I had longed for my current pregnancy, this baby to adopt, and there was family excitement, there was also nervousness among all who loved me. I was 39 and overweight, and it had not been long since our family had been through a challenging time. These were reasonable and appropriate concerns.

Of course, given the circumstances and since we were not matched to Xia, the logical question was, "Should we proceed with a Chinese adoption, in that the government was working on another match for us?" We shared our confusion with the adoption agency but by no means ruled out adoption. We just had to stop and think . . . and feel.

I was at work when an email arrived from the adoption agency. "Julie, you and Bill have been matched." I saw that there were attachments. Should I open? I could not resist, click. There was the face of my little girl. She sat in a baby walker with a little printed outfit. She looked up at the camera with an inquisitive look. I immediately forwarded the email to Bill.

It was agreed that I would write down every one of the family's fears. With yellow legal pad in hand, Bill and I met with my OB doctor. She listened intently and answered every question with much thought and education. In her opinion, if I traveled between 20 and 23 weeks' gestation and took care, I would be at no greater risk if traveling to China. This dear doctor helped bring both of our girls into our world. I will never stop being thankful for the time that she, the obstetrician, gave to us.

Forest trail with stepping stones.
Photo courtesy of Susan Hilliard.

Bill and I walked and talked, night after night, on a trail at the park near our home. The heart question, "How can we not proceed with the adoption? I honestly felt connected to each child. The one on the other side of the globe, even though not Xia, was as much mine as was the little one that I was carrying. Each precious. Each a gift and each with incredible purpose all wrapped up with our life purpose. I just knew. I had a knowing that is very difficult to explain but yet was solid.

***

I reached out to the woman who had let me know about the other couple who requested to adopt Xia. She let me know that they were traveling for her soon. "When the time is right and with her permission, may I have her email address?" It was given to me. I was ready to say goodbye to Xia.

Hoping that I would not be perceived as a stalker, I reached out to Xia's adopted mom. I learned a little about the relationship between Xia and her first daughter and felt so good about the love she would receive. In the conversation, the mom commented that she lived in Pennsylvania. Months later, as a final act of closure, I took all my pictures of Xia, the video and medical reports and placed them in a pretty cloth-covered box. I explained to Xia's mom that I had prepared these treasures for her. It is understood among those who adopt that any piece of information about the child's life before is cherished. I acknowledged that she had mentioned living in Pennsylvania. I explained, "My sister will be visiting from Pittsburgh. I could send the items back with her. Are you by any odd chance anywhere near?"

She replied, "Yes, I live in Pittsburgh!"

"Wow, my sister is near the airport and works in Moon," I explained.

She replied, "I live in Moon and work near the airport."

***

My oh my, how beautiful! I had been given everything that I needed for acceptance and peace, and to move forward. Who could have imagined such an unfolding? I closed up the box and gave it to my sister. They did in fact meet. Susan gave the box to Xia's mother. Although these items represent the path to Lacy, it felt good to place them where they belonged.

Ironically, I later learned that Xia had been in a dance class taught by my cousin. Two families from this side of the world had a miraculous connection formed on the other side of the world by one little face among a sea of children. Some call it coincidental; others say it is synchronicity; I call it a miracle.

CHAPTER FOURTEEN

MEETING LACY

In 2002, Bill, Ben and I were on a flight to Beijing, and I was 21 weeks' gestation. This was not long after 9-11, so the traveling atmosphere was rather intense. Ben even worked through his emotions to travel without his Squishy Puppy in fear that it may be taken by security. We toured for several days before flying to the providence of Xinjiang. Wherever we went, crowds gathered around Ben. Some called him, "Harry Potter," because he had glasses and was about the age of the movie character. His hair, in contrast to Harry, was very blond. That color also drew much attention. With giggles, we agreed that we should have charged for the many pictures taken with him.

On the Great Wall, I particularly remembered the people laughing and pointing at Bill, who had shorts on. This was very odd sight in the fall in China.

All was fascinating! I was in awe of the strong knees that Chinese of all ages must have because so many squatted as they relaxed and talked. I would have just toppled on over!

A few days later, we were in a hotel room near the Adobe Desert and the old Silk Road in China. Our guide arrived with Lacy on her hip. Lacy was 17 months old. I kissed her little hands, and she leaned out of our guide's arms and into the arms of her 11-year-old big brother. He beamed with pride and held her very securely. Throughout the years of their relationship that followed, Ben was always able to comfort Lacy. Many times, she was shifted to his back, and he carried her. While wading in a creek and afraid of the water spiders, Lacy rode on his back with no fear at all. When she was 9 and no longer so small, on a museum trip that she found frightening . . . on his back she went. He had a gift for making her feel safe.

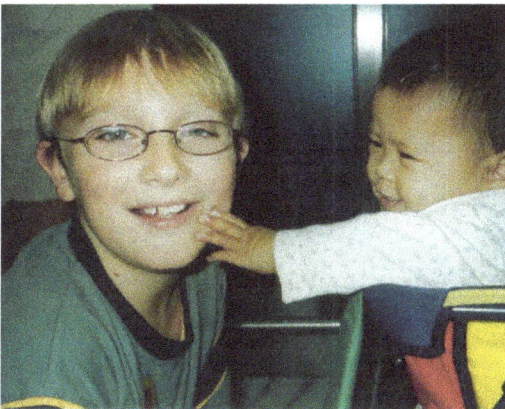

Ben and Baby Lacy in China.

Over the next week and a half, we all learned a lot about each other. Each day was exciting and special. We had brought a small, deflated beach ball as a toy. One of the adoption groups recommended that toy due to the ease of carrying it while traveling. We began a game of passing the inflated ball back and forth while saying the name of the one receiving the ball. Lacy, Ben, Mommy, Daddy. Almost immediately, Lacy learned to recognize her name and Ben was given a modified name by her—Bubba.

We jumped at the opportunity to tour Shihezi Child Welfare Institute. The ride in the small bus was long and very bumpy. Some of the roads were dirt. The bumps were at times so big that we actually lifted off the seats. An uneasiness began to wash over me. After all, I was 5 months pregnant. Our guide, Sophie, sat on the seat behind me. She took Lacy to hold and put her hand on my shoulders. I believe that she was very concerned too. There was nothing that we could do but continue to our destination. Sophie seemed to be fussing at the driver as she stayed connected to me.

Finally, we arrived. The orphanage director and several nurses in white lab jackets came to greet us. The nurses were filled with joy to see Lacy. I believe they loved her and were very happy to "check us out." I am forever thankful for their care. The director seemed proud to show us a new truck and to point across a yard of dirt to an older wooden building. The guide translated that the move from this old building had been made just a few years before. The new building was made of cinderblocks. We were invited to a meeting room that had sofas and a table of fruit for us. We had been advised not to eat any of the fruit. Our bodies, being from America, would not be accustomed to the biome of the area and we may get sick. I felt extreme pressure to show my gratitude and participate in the hospitality. I put a grape in my mouth. The guide quickly said, "Spit it out!" Which I did. Awkward.

The director asked us if we would like to take a tour. We said yes and thanked him. It was so cold that we kept our winter coats on. Snow was on the mountaintops that ran alongside the sandy city and the month was October. As we were leaving the meeting room, staff kept coming to Ben. It seemed that each person gave Ben a fruit. One gave him a carton of milk. He was the star attraction everywhere we went! Ben repeatedly said, "Xie Xie." It means thank you. As we walked, we had not noticed that Ben had been hiding the fruit in the sleeves of his big winter coat. Well, that was a pretty good approach to carrying so many small items!

After we saw the small kitchen with tofu soaking in deep pans and a noodle maker, we were shown the room where Lacy had lived. There were little beds in lines. We passed a long room with little potty chairs in a row and saw a very small play room. We came to a room of older children. The director placed his hand on the heads of two. He said, "These children are in the adoption process. Lacy was just the fourth child to be adopted from this province." He explained that when the children were old enough, they were taken to pick cotton. This helped cover the expenses of care. The director and staff seemed to be doing all they could to provide for all these little ones in a system so different from what we had become accustomed to in America.

When the tour was complete, the smiling women kissed Lacy goodbye, and we got back in the bumpy bus. We followed the orphanage director in his new, little truck to the nearby hospital. The hospital looked very different from what we Americans typically picture in our minds. He showed us the concrete steps where Lacy had been abandoned and found by a nurse. Lacy was estimated to be 20 days old, wrapped in a quilt and in need of minor but life-saving gastrointestinal surgery. The director explained, "A charitable organization paid for her medical care." The initial repair of a birth defect saved her life. She also had an extra thumb that required surgery two months after traveling home to Winston-Salem.

Someone, probably a parent or a grandparent, carefully wrapped the little baby and left her where care could be received. I imagine the courage it must have taken. We were told that medical care in China is for the rich.

While driving into the city, we passed rows and rows of lean-tos. They had dirt floors, I believe. The director said, "Lacy would have been born at home."

The one-child policy of the time made it a crime to have a second child; yet it was illegal to abandon a child. So many hard decisions and sacrifices. Much was also complicated by the cultural preference for boys and the responsibility assigned to sons regarding the care of aging parents. I believe that Lacy's biological family positioned her for the best chance. I hope that we have been the answer to love's prayer.

We all loaded back up to go to a lunch with a "government official." The bumpy bus took us to a restaurant in the city. We were greeted by young women in traditional Chinese dress. They guided us up some stairs and to a private dining room. There was a large round table. In the middle of the table was a lazy Susan.

With smiles and nods, pretty waitresses began to help us remove our coats. Pa-pa-pa-pa-pa . . . orange, purple and golden fruit hit the floor and rolled in all directions. Ben sheepishly looked over the top of his glasses and said, "I'm sorry."

Beside him was a stunned young lady holding his coat! Suddenly, beautiful silk dresses scurried around the room chasing the rolling fruit. The dresses were cut straight, so the poor ladies had to contort themselves to reach the floor. And the official was due in the room any second! Ben had graciously accepted their fruit gifts but had not tried to eat any of them.

The official arrived and was accompanied by his grown daughter. I asked the official, "What would you like us to teach Lacy about her home city?"

He answered, "Let her know that it is a beautiful place." He had a very kind and gentle manner. He thanked us for providing for Lacy, and we thanked him for her care. He asked us the type of work that we did.

Through our translator/guide we explained, "Bill works as the administrator of a nursing home for the elderly, and I oversee group homes for people with intellectual disabilities."

The official looked puzzled and sincere. He asked, "How do you do that? How do you pay for the care of your people?"

I answered, "We have a system in America in which everyone who pays taxes is contributing a portion of the care. This is used to pay for many who are unable to care for themselves."

He seemed amazed.

Oh, this is what is so different and special about America, I thought.

While I know that America has had many systems of compassion, there is also a history of pain and suffering. The beauty and the ugly is all part of what is. America once slaughtered Native Americans and kidnapped and enslaved African people. Still remaining are many who are hungry and forgotten. There are still systems of racism and struggles with inequality.

During this conversation with the official on this day, however, I felt an overwhelming appreciation for and connection to all who have given their lives and suffered for the removal of barriers; a bringing together; prioritizing compassion; care and support; and a determination to be fair with a principle that honors human value.

In this kind and humble connection between people from two countries, the care of the elderly and the disabled was highlighted. I wished that the children at the orphanage had days filled with education instead of long, hot hours of picking cotton. I wish that the little ones with blue lips had the best cardiologist available to ease their suffering little bodies. I know that the official had the same desire. We all continue on our journey with the hope of finding paths of love.

***

Upon returning to America, a welcome party greeted us! There was so much love and excitement.

Lacy walked within a month. The next month she had her surgery for the extra thumb. Four months after our arrival home with Lacy, Sophie was born and was given the name of the kind guide who gave love and care to me and my baby through the simple act of placing her hand on my shoulder during a very bumpy ride. Life was a whirlwind of wonder, fulfillment and exhaustion.

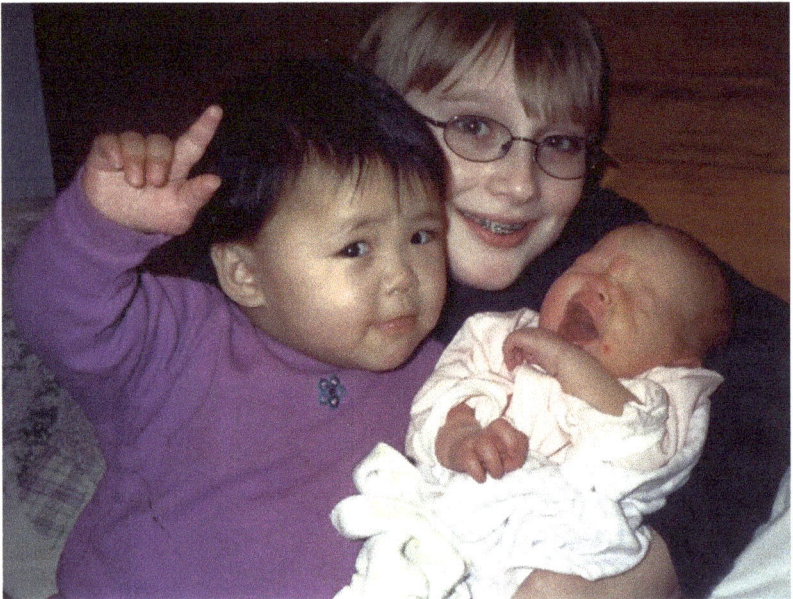

Favorite picture of all time, 2003.

CHAPTER FIFTEEN

EPICENTER

The first officer took me aside. "Ma'am, I need you to look at me and really listen." He leaned down to make sure that our eyes met and again firmly and a bit louder said, "Look at my eyes and listen carefully to what I am saying. Focus on me, ma'am. Ma'am, are there firearms in the home?"

"No."

"Ma'am, you must remove anything that could be used by you or any of your family to harm oneself. Ma'am, do you understand?"

"Yes, sir, we do not have any weapons."

"Ma'am, we will stay as long as you need us."

"Sir, he didn't call me. My baby . . . he didn't call me."

***

My family now belongs to the deep, deep loss-connected people who lived across all history, lands and cultures of the world, who have been spiritually scooped up from a life of the familiar and abruptly dropped into an existence of unfamiliar lostness. I imagine that many have the shared experience of mustering the strength to communicate and manage logistics while residing in the world of spinning thoughts . . . bouncing between actual memory and imagination, perseverating on words and facial expressions. These early days are lived in a fog of survival.

Bill's sister, Joyce, stayed with us for the first few days and then my sister, Susan. They took charge of the daily details. My brothers, sisters-in-law, nieces, nephews, aunt, uncles, cousins, friends, neighbors . . . all came to us and piece by piece constructed, to the very best of their ability, a nest of love and care. This, too, sent a powerful ripple of love throughout.

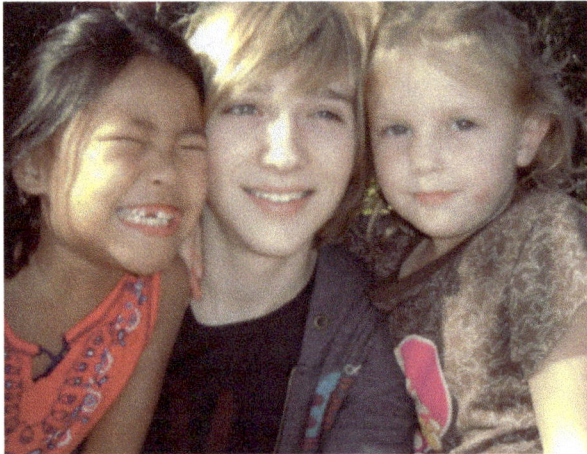

A fun day at Reynolda Park.

For us, confusion and helplessness engulfed our front yard—the epicenter of our crippling sorrow. Also present was a mighty rippling power of kindness, help and love. The brutal and the sacred were delicately woven together.

The day after Ben died, we heard movement downstairs. We went down to find Lacy standing by the door, dressed for school, holding the lunch bag that she had packed herself. She was desperate for some resemblance to normal life. She was taken to school by our neighbor.

CHAPTER SIXTEEN
CHECKING IN

Every now and then, Sophie passed by with Donna to walk in the neighborhood.

I kept an eye on Lacy and Sophie's safety, but the truth is, I could not offer them the comfort and care that they needed at this time. They lost their brother and in a way, lost their father on the same day. I gave all that I had by making sure someone else whom we loved and trusted and who loved each of them, came to them. With my focus on managing to breathe, I could not be there for them.

If only I could have held Ben while he suffered; if only I could have let him lean on me for hope when he had none; if only I could have helped; if only I had seen; if only I had not seen him as one who had held everything together with strength and wisdom, if only I had been known to his friends and teachers who might have reached out to me; if only there was not FERPA—Family

Educational Rights and Privacy Act—I might have learned that he was missing school. If only, if only, if only, if only . . .

If only I could have held Sophie and Lacy during this trauma. If only I could have stroked their hair, made space for crying, wiped their tears, screamed, sobbed and named the unspeakable alongside them, sheltering them in my love . . . but it was not to be. They had my love every minute during this loss and forever, as did Ben, but I was not present for them—for a mother who would give anything to protect her children. It is not in self-judgment; it is just the reality. I have been told that depression or another serious crisis on the part of the parent always represents abandonment for the child. I was grief stricken. And while I know that I did my best, it makes me so very sad.

Chapter Seventeen

EMPTY

Painfully, a huge piece of the information puzzle lay before me on the second or third day after Ben's death. This information took my breath and has been a haunting to deal with. I went downstairs to his apartment in our house. We had been using the downstairs refrigerator as overflow for the gifts of meals. I passed his room, stopped and looked back.

After my mom moved out of the apartment to a senior living community, Ben was offered the space she had occupied. He was a high school upperclassman, and with the upstairs full of lively young girls, it seemed perfect for him to have some separate but connected space. He picked out the colors, and together we painted the bedroom and bathroom.

But today, I did not see the familiar picture of the earth that he had hanging on the wall, his various decorations or books. The tops of all of the furniture were clear. I felt the all-too-familiar flood of adrenaline throughout my being, and nausea hit my stomach. In a state of fear, I opened his drawers and then his closet. He had emptied the room. During our Norman Rockwell spring break experience of joy and family connection, Ben was completely clearing his room. He did not want to leave us with this burdensome task. *Why had I not been downstairs to notice? My God,* I remembered, *the week was so busy that we did not prepare his room as we normally did. What would the outcome have been if I had connected these dots?*

Ben in a self-portrait.

On the wall, as it had been since the summer before, were words. Ben had previously taped off the letters and painted over the wall. So where the tape was then removed, it left these words:

ALL FLESH IS GRASS.

When he had completed the painting, I asked, Ben, "What is that and what does it mean?"

Ben said, "It just means that everything has a season. I thought it was neat."

I remember thinking, *This is a little weird, but Ben loves words. This fits.* It sounded familiar. Later that summer I looked it up. it came from Isaiah 40:6 KJV. "All flesh is grass and all the goodliness thereof is a flower of the field. The grass withers and the flower fades, but the word of God stands forever."

CHAPTER EIGHTEEN

NO MORE BULL

Our house was full of supportive people. Food was being brought in at a steady pace. I was thankful for the love and care. I could barely get a bite down, but I ate here and there. We continued to feed Bill with protein shakes. One day, in mustering all the ability that he could, Bill managed to pick up our sushi platter. He turned it over and wrote across the bottom with a Sharpie,

LAST SUSHI NIGHT, 3/15/2013.

My dear friend and coworker, Bonnie, arrived. She rubbed Lavender on my arms, put a turquoise necklace on me—representing healing—and hugged me. She looked at me and said, "Let's get out of here!"

I shook my head yes.

We began to walk around the neighborhood. It did me good to get out of all the activity for a few minutes. As we walked, I said something like, "Well, maybe something good will come from this." I continued to speak with a sickening Pollyanna whitewash of all the tragedy.

Bonnie stopped walking, turned to me and wisely said, "No!" She put her hands on my cheeks, pulling me to face her. "No, Julie, stop it! This is f_____ horrible! Say it! You need to say it! I was jolted to a reality and truth. Yes, it truly was f_____ horrible, and I said it! I needed to say it. Somehow, I don't think that I would have had a prayer of putting the shattered pieces back together had I not expressed the raw truth.

CHAPTER NINETEEN

A DIFFERENT CRY

The moments and days after Ben left were filled with I'm sorrys and thank yous. Our home became the gathering place. Many arrived to give and receive comfort. While I was existing in this external world of activity, my internal world, in a sense, was numb. But not really numb because I felt everything. I was in a constant state of reliving every word, look and sound that occurred from the moment that the "life after" began—ruminating over and over, spinning in my mind. My words and actions, however, continued—checking on my girls and mom, making sure someone was caring for them, ensuring Bill was safe and that someone was assigned to him. I kept notes of who did what, answered the phone, made logistical plans and maintained communication.

It was in the shower, alone, and in the warmth of water, that my roles and responsibilities were temporarily cleared. The intensity of emotion was unfamiliar, heaving and stealing my breath, while giving voice to the agonizing cry rising up and out from every cell of this mother body. Just me—my heart, my mind, my soul. My vulnerable being— raw, naked, real. Me as a human, shattered and displaced to an unfamiliar existence. Anguish.

Storm clouds reflect the intensity
and darkness of the emotions.
Photo courtesy of Susan Hilliard.

The loss, from the death of Ben, produced an engulfing effect that in no way resembled the other losses of my life . . . my father, brother, grandparents, aunts, uncles and pets. Now we belong, as others have said, to a club that no one chooses to join. I was bound to mothers throughout the world and throughout all time who lost a child.

***

Months passed, but the sorrow remained. My response was to seek and accept help in any way that I could. I read everything I could find about losing a child to suicide and obtained individual and group counseling specific to suicide loss. I grabbed onto every life raft that I could reach for. One suggestion that I had heard was to draw where in one's body the pain is felt. I sat down with paper and a pack of colored pencils.

After sketching a bit of a face, I determined that I felt the pain in my abdomen. I began striking the paper harshly—at first with sadness that turned to anger. The marks became darker and more erratic. There, on the paper, I had created a ball of fury. I was beginning to learn the necessity of facing the emotions that are perceived as negative emotions—deep, dark and hateful: anger, prejudice, judgment and blame. I had previously struggled with a perception that these feelings were wrong, that of weakness. I still struggle with this. But if stuffed down or aside, the unexpressed pain will come out in unhealthy ways. As my Aunt Sue has taught me, the entire array of feelings need to be examined and accepted as the condition of being human. They must be worked with, journaled about and shared with those who will not judge us so that we will not act them out on others. As she explains, we are not living our truth when we do not face our pain and fear. After creating the image of complex emotions, I felt a release of sorts. After wiping my tears, sitting with my thoughts for a bit, I returned to the painful cluster of feelings. From the ball, my hands, without thought, began the sweeping strokes of growing strong roots, new life, rainbows and butterflies.

Pain must first be faced.
Art by the grieving author.

We need not judge our feelings. We must work with them. From that work, good can and will come.

CHAPTER TWENTY

HIGH SCHOOL

The high school years brought transformation for Ben from an awkward teenager who lacked in confidence to one who shined. He transformed into a handsome, trim teen with long hair and a free-spirit way about him.

At the beginning of each school year, Ben and I followed a routine. We learned over the years that confusion is reduced if I began the student, teacher, parental relationship as follows: "Ben has a 504 educational plan because he has mild cerebral palsy. His plan allows the accommodation of using a laptop in order to write and complete assignments. He is independent in making modifications to make it easy on you. For example, he often color codes and prints work or can submit through a flash drive or email. Please determine what works best for you, and he will do it that way."

I do not remember whether it was in the 11th or 12th grade year, but the response of the new teacher opened a window into Ben's world of which I had no idea. I knew that he was a deep thinker, but I had no clue that he was a writer. Per established routine, when Ben introduced himself to be followed by my elevator speech, one teacher said with a glow of respect, excitement and a soft honoring voice, "Ben Wood, I have read your writings and am very glad to meet you and have you in my class."

Ben at Lake Junaluska dam.
Photo courtesy of Susan Hilliard.

I did a double take. I played along, but the talk in my mind was, *Ben is a writer? What in the world has he written?"* Ben never wanted to draw attention to himself. I had no idea that he had this gift. It was challenging to get him to share with me things he had written. He seemed embarrassed. I know that had he lived, he would have put amazing insight into this world.

Later in the year, Ben was surprised to learn that his writing had placed in a county-wide Reflections Award contest. His teacher had entered one of Ben's assignments on his behalf. This award represented an important message to him by saying, "You are valuable and have much to contribute to the world." After his death I learned how important this award was to him. This was a marker in his life.

Ben experiencing joy with friends.

Chapter Twenty-One

DISMANTLING SANCTUARY

After Doug and Beverly left as the youth leaders, there were challenges in finding a new youth leader for our church. Ben continued to represent the church as a district youth representative and served as a delegate to the Western North Carolina annual conference of the United Methodist church.

Finally, the staff parish committee arranged interviews for a new youth leader. After meeting with the committee, each candidate would meet with the youth group. There were several immediate dismissals. Time seemed to move slowly until there was a recommendation from someone on staff. A new youth leader was selected. Although he was from a more fundamental denomination, he was described as very proactive, knowledgeable and enthusiastic. In addition, he sang and played a keyboard. The committee thought the kids would love him. The kids met him and thought, *Well, he seems okay.* Ben agreed and said the man's wife seemed really nice, friendly and kind.

Soon into the relationship, the wife told my husband, "Ben is so clever and funny. What a great kid!"

Early into this new relationship, the group did a local mission project, painting some of the buildings on the campus of residential services for children. Since Ben did not eat meat, not knowing if the new youth leader knew to make accommodations, we sent some food just to be safe. The first sign of a problem unfolded on this project. The youth director told Ben that anyone who did not eat meat had some serious issues. Ben came home and said, "Something is really wrong here."

A wonderful and dedicated adult helper also clashed with the new leader and found many of his comments unacceptable. This dear assistant quickly saw that he simply could not work with this new guy on the scene. About a year later he told me, "I am so sorry that I let this man run me off. Maybe If I had stayed, I could have made a difference."

Although he was not in any way involved in the later trauma Ben suffered, his caring was very comforting.

***

Not too long after the painting mission project, Ben came home from a youth group and said, "Mom, he really does not believe that women should have leadership roles in the church." We were concerned. Ben added, "He also seems to think that Oprah Winfrey is part of an anti-Christian cult." I notified the pastor.

The church secretary, who is a beautiful soul, said to me, "Julie, try to give him a chance." Our concerns did not fit her experience.

What the new leader presented to the staff was not consistent with what we were seeing. From what we could gather, the new leader behaved so kindly to them that they were loyal to him. The truth is, he did have wonderful qualities. But, these qualities did not diminish the impact of the harmful messages that he often delivered.

Ben said, "The leader stated that the reason war continues in the Middle East is due to the sins of the fathers. I responded by talking about multiple reasons, such as the American redistribution of land after WWII and other historical contributing factors to the modern conflict." Ben's points were taken as disrespect and a challenge. The leader became infuriated. Ben said, "We were not allowed to eat dinner until the leader felt that we accepted his explanations."

I talked with this leader myself on several occasions about our concerns. I usually felt as though we had understood each other. I always left feeling that things would be different. But truthfully, I don't know now what was real or was spin and manipulation. He expressed displeasure about Ben's attitude and lack of respect for him as a leader. I told him we were not happy about what he was teaching.

Later, there was an outdoor picnic at the church shelter. As the youth prepared, Ben and one of his female friends went to get something from behind the scout hut. Ben said that as they walked back, one of the kids said to the leader, "I thought that a boy and a girl weren't supposed to go back there."

The leader responded, "That is Ben Wood. Nothing is going to happen back there." And then he laughed.

I met with him again. I told him, "I realize that some could suspect Ben as gay, but he may or may not be. We don't know. But I can acknowledge that he does not fit into a classic masculine role. Do you have a problem with that?"

He said, "Oh, I've worked with homosexuals in the past."

I told him, "We are all learning life lessons each day, but I hope you can see that your current way of interacting and teaching is not acceptable." We seemed to end on a good note.

Bill and I shared our discomforts with our Sunday school class who tenderly affirmed support for us, and then we met with the pastor. I laid out all our concerns. He seemed to understand and committed to be involved.

However, this tension continued to build over the course of a year. Slowly, Ben was quietly removed from each leadership role in which he served.

The parents of a friend of Ben planned to get a divorce. The friend went to the leader for support. Instead, she received a cruel and fear-based preaching that divorce was a sin and her parents would be judged. She confided in Ben who reacted with fury. Several friends left the group, but Ben was determined to stay with it and change what was happening. Ben loved what this group had been before the new leader came and wanted to save it.

All of this occurred while some kids and even some parents idolized the youth leader. One of his endearing qualities was that he seemed to be taking some under his wing, especially a young fellow who was in need of a father figure. Notes of appreciation for his dedication, care and leadership were published in the newsletter. Although contradictory in appearance and outcome, each person's experience with this youth leader was true for that person. The summary of how interactions made each feel formed an opinion of the impact this individual had on all. It may be human nature to generalize our own interpretation of experiences to assume that it is the experience of everyone else. We've all seen it. This contradiction in opinions was very confusing to us, and we felt hurt that the leadership of the church and some of the other families involved with the youth group did not see. His behavior felt so foreign and appalling to us. Yet others could not understand or see our concern. The good actions, which were there, seemed to hide the harm being done to Ben.

Ben, first year of college.
Photo courtesy of Kimberly LaBombard.

During this period of time, confusion really set in; we could see our loved and safe church shifting. This man had quite a following, and others were blind to the undertones. There were direct and indirect messages that he was ranking human value based on theology of a tyrannical God. Then he would sing songs of praise and love with others singing along and participating. The church that we had known for about fifteen years had never looked this way.

This was a time of much worry, conflict and attempts to make good come out of this situation. I was so Pollyanna-like. I thought that we all could talk our way to everyone learning and growing. That is not what happened.

We were very rooted in this particular church community. The Sunday school class was filled with dear and trusted friends. We were journeying through life together. There had been births, deaths, miscarriages, adoptions, lost jobs, so much of life. All of life's challenges were acknowledged, discussed and reframed into a message of faith and hope as we shared this circle of friends. Here there was a garden that fed the hungry, a homeless ministry and an orphan care team. It was a beautiful and loving place. However, fear and judgment seeped in and resulted in a paralysis and harm.

If this kind of shift can creep in and take hold in a place such as this, it can slither in anywhere to distort and transform a place of love to an instrument of hate all costumed under the misused cover of God. How God must weep in sorrow!

CHAPTER TWENTY-TWO

THE SLASHING OF A SOUL

The day was ordinary. Even though evening was approaching, the sun shone brightly. Bill was mowing the grass in the front yard and was just past a group of three small trees in front of our bay window. The girls and I were doing normal summer evening things. I don't remember exactly, but I may have been preparing dinner. Ben was not with us. He had gone to the church for an extra youth meeting to complete the final planning for a mission trip. It would be only a few days until the youth group would load the church bus and head to the mission site.

Although the group had increasingly become a nest of conflict, confusion and stress, Ben really wanted to see this trip through. He loved helping paint, build porches or whatever else would benefit someone in need. "This is what the church is all about," he told me. He also loved the camaraderie, teamwork and fun. He had committed to the mission trip.

The teachings of the new leader were upsetting and contradictory to anything that Ben had been taught. Our meetings with church leadership had been supportive and understanding, yet we could not see any improvement in the behavior of this charismatic youth leader. We agreed that after the trip, a decision would be made. Should we leave a group that had been so dear or tough it out and try to help open eyes? Ben, Bill and I had each commented, "If we run away and leave, it will not change." Later, I wondered why we thought it was appropriate to step in as the sacrificial lambs. If only we had recognized the need to protect ourselves, our family and especially our dear, brilliant, sensitive, social justice-seeking son.

***

As I walked into the family room about ninety minutes after Ben had left, Ben's car caught my eye through the bay window. It was fast and abrupt as it whipped into our driveway. *Something is wrong! He is home early.* I quickly walked to the front door. As I opened the door, Ben ran up the steps to our front porch. The intensity was palpable. The beautiful green eyes of my 16-year-old child locked directly into mine. Tears filled his lids in a pool that was just about to spill over. His cheeks were flushed, his breathing rapid and his lips . . . oh his lips quivered as he formed words with great effort and despite the contortion of his face on the verge of crying.

"He has yelled at me for an hour!" Ben said. "He made my friends say they were not comfortable with me and that I was going to hell. 'I'm sorry for anything I have done,' I told him. He said that he did not believe me."

The agony, pain, abandonment and devastating betrayal fell on our home like a heavy, suffocating toxic blanket.

I told the girls that I had to go to the church and for them to stay with Ben. I grabbed my keys and intercepted Bill with the lawnmower and said we have to go to the church now. He turned off the mower, took the keys and got into the car. While Bill drove the seven-minute route to the church, I called my dear friend, Casey, and said, "I need you. Please come to the church. He has done something else to Ben and it is awful." I said, "I have to call the senior pastor. Can you get me the parsonage number?" I was honestly afraid of what was about to happen. Her husband looked up the number while we were talking, and I called the pastor. I said, "I need you. I need you to come to the church now!"

We walked in the back of the church where a group of parents who were supposed to be chaperoning in the basement youth room, stood outside the basement door in the hallway.

"Who was in the room? Who was protecting Ben?" I uncharacteristically blurted.

One dear friend said with a soft voice, "The leader asked us to leave."

I said, "He has done something horrible." My voice shook and tears streamed down my face.

Ben's friend later told me that while we were at the church, she was on the phone with Ben. She had not made it to youth that night. She said, "This is the first time in my life that my best friend—since we were in the church nursery together—sobbed uncontrollably! If only I had been there."

"Why have we let this son of a bitch stay at our church?" The words literally burst from Bill's mouth.

The parents appeared shocked and knew that they should have stayed in the room. The youth leader was still in the youth room with the other children. None of this felt real, and I wondered, *How could this be happening. How? How could this happen in such a loving and sacred place?*

We were soon in the pastor's office. My dear friend arrived and waited just outside the office door after hugging Bill and me. The associate pastor was already there, and the senior pastor rushed through the door. The associate pastor explained that he was at the youth meeting for part of the conversation, but that he was asked to leave by the youth leader "due to a need to deeply discuss feelings privately as a group."

In walked the youth leader.

"What have you done?" I was whispering emphatically.

He answered, "Ben has a bad attitude, and the other kids don't want him to go on the trip."

"Ben said that he apologized," I said.

"He didn't mean it," the youth leader barked.

"You don't like him because he is gay," I said.

He glared and shouted, "Homosexuality is an abomination to God!"

His facial expression, tone and words were so degrading. I said, "What if God is teaching you, showing you something different, peeling back the layers of the onion so that you can see God's child?"

With belligerence, he said, "I know everything that I need to know."

I pointed toward him and firmly asked, "What about Open Hearts, Open Minds and Open Doors, the Methodist motto?"

The youth leader said, "I don't care about that!"

A commercial on TV showing the "radical hospitality" of the United Methodist church that ended with "Open Hearts, Open Minds and Open Doors" continued to air. I used to be very proud to be a part of something that beautiful and Jesus-like. The commercials oozed compassion, non-judgmentalism, warmth and safety. Yet, this youth leader did not care.

The two pastors watched paralyzed until there was an exhausted end road to the conversation. The senior pastor said, "Let's pray."

I do not remember hearing a word.

We all left.

Casey walked out with us and lovingly asked, "How did you stay in there?" We were in complete shock.

We got home to hug Ben. We told him that the youth leader was wrong. "He showed how ignorant he is, but this is nothing about you, Ben." Ben was completely empty and his affect was now flat. He just wanted to go to bed.

For Ben, the candle of good and kind in the world was blown out with each hateful word directed toward him. Extinguished. I do not believe that he ever felt safe, outside of a close trusted group, again.

Ben standing alone on a mountaintop.
Photo courtesy of Evelyn Pierce, a college friend.

Chapter Twenty-Three

BEHIND THE CLOSED
YOUTH ROOM DOORS

This is what I learned happened behind the doors when I received accounts from Ben, a friend of his and another youth in the room,

Chairs were pulled into a circle. The Associate Pastor cofacilitated a discussion around faith and group relationships. After the Associate Pastor left, the youth leader began the dismantling process. The sanctuary of Ben Wood was disassembled with surgical precision. A lesson was delivered. The topic: homosexuality. The stones: you are disgusting, shameful, unlovable, an abomination, dirty and not deserving of God's love.

How horrible Ben must have felt to sit in this seat, in a circle, knowing that his presence most likely motivated the lesson! While Ben had never acknowledged being gay, he advocated for the acceptance of LGBTQ+, was passionate about the rights of individuals and never *denied* being gay. He simply was non-committal at this time. He probably had talked to close friends, but I do not know. How uncomfortable each youth member must have felt, knowing Ben was gay and was now being discussed and that it gave opportunity for the leader to put Ben in a vulnerable position! How much self-control did it take for Ben to sit there so that he could complete the mission trip? How much dedication he demonstrated to his friends, to his church and to the stranger whom he was committed to help! I wonder if he let out a breath of relief when the formal lesson had ended. My baby. His journey had already been so very difficult. My beautiful, beautiful, sensitive and loving son, whom I respected and cherished so very much. How, how could such evil have entered our church through this one man?

The emotional flogging, however, had just begun. The lesson was over and the personal ambush was underway.

"Who here is not comfortable with Ben going on the mission trip?" the youth leader demanded.

Ben sat in silence. Judged. A life-long friend raised his hand, and he was then joined by others. The friend later explained that he thought that the leader was addressing Ben's prior spoken disagreement and challenging of the youth leader's teachings. He had no idea where the conversation was going. From that point on, the conversation was like a runaway train. That very evening the friend called to apologize to Ben. Ben forgave him and understood the pressure he was under.

The leader said, "I know. We all know that YOU are gay, Ben." He began the next phase of destruction. Each child was asked, one by one, around the circle, "Do you understand that Ben is going to hell?"

The kids felt extreme pressure to say yes. So they did.

He continued, "Ben you will go to hell!" He was shouting. "You are no representation of Christ; therefore, you may not go on this trip. You are not worthy of being a part of this youth group."

***

That was it. Each of us in our family and others were picked up from the life that we were leading and placed on a completely different, dark and lonely path. The youth leader made his mark . . . his target was taken down to never feel whole and safe again.

Ben and Tiffany, lifelong friends.

After an hour, Ben left the room and drove home. A friend told me that after Ben left, the youth began to speak up and say, "Ben is our friend." "We have never cared whether he was gay or not." Some of these children were as young as rising sixth graders and the oldest were high school seniors. It was too late. It was finished.

CHAPTER TWENTY-FOUR

CONFUSION

We were consumed with confusion. There were complicated emotional layers regarding our relationship with Christianity, the church and specifically, the United Methodist church. All that we had learned through all that we experienced and that which grounded us had been removed from the current reality. Our brains tried to make sense of what could not be made sense of. Even our sense of self-identity was in question.

Several generations of Bill's family life were woven in a United Methodist church. Even as a young acolyte, Bill passed a Sunday school class door with a plaque: William Wood Memorial Class . . . his name, his grandfather's name.

For me, I was the daughter of a United Methodist pastor starting with being brought home as a newborn to the parsonage across from the church . . . not our home, but the church's home.

We moved every four years until my dad's last appointment. When the church's annual meeting took place, we vacationed at Lake Junaluska in Western North Carolina. I was shaped and formed by this experience in the role of a preacher's child.

It wasn't until recent years that I learned why the property was named Lake Junaluska. The reason was to memorialize a man treated unjustly in a manner that created widespread tragedy. Lake Junaluska was named after Chief Junaluska. Andrew Jackson claimed this Cherokee as a brother. The chief dedicated his tribe to fight alongside Jackson and saved Jackson's life through an incredibly creative and risky plan. After the Cherokee took such deep sacrifices, Jackson became president. He sent Chief Junaluska, his family and tribe on the devastating Trail of Tears. He told his "brother," "There is nothing I can do for you." Years later, the betrayal was acknowledged, a memorial and museum were created at his grave and the United Methodist Assembly was named after him. Not only is this the place where I went throughout my childhood, but it is also the place where Ben later attended conference as a youth delegate. This is also where he heard bitter debates on homosexuality. Bill and I were not in attendance and had no idea what he had been exposed to.

I was betrayed by everything that I ever knew to be good—the teachings of Jesus, of God who had constructed a solid grounding for me to live. *What is reality?* I wondered. *Was I lied to then or am I lied to now?* The bursting of illusions was devastating.

Church Directory
Family portrait, 2008.
Photographer unknown.

We shared our pain with lay leaders and clergy who implied there were misunderstandings that could be worked through. A church member said, "I understand that Ben was being a teenager, making disparaging remarks against the leader on Facebook and disrespecting him."

What? It seemed that to find some justification was a way some avoided the truth. The bigger challenge would be to face the confusion and work out of the paralysis of contradictory messages. Church . . . now represented a big fat lie! Others were devastated and hurt alongside us. So much pain, so much unnecessary pain.

We were in sorrowful grief . . . disenfranchised grief. A grief that was not acknowledged or understood and was dismissed by the church leadership and some of the congregation—for not taking action. They just could not see the severity of the harm. The betrayal and abandonment created a loss of great magnitude. And just think, poor Ben had to look at his bewildered parents and somehow feel, *What have I caused?*

My God . . . how did we find ourselves in this situation?

"Jesus Loves the Little Children, All the Children of the World," "Jesus Loves Me. This I Know." These and the Golden Rule are the foundational lessons of my family and church. In a United Methodist church youth room, the message was distorted to Ben: "You are unacceptable, unwanted and not a representation of Christ. And you are not worthy to belong . . . you are abandoned."

Lessons from early childhood were based on Scripture:

> *Before I formed you in the womb, I knew you, and before you were born, I consecrated you.*
> *–Jeremiah 1:5 ESV*
> *You made all the delicate, inner parts of my body and knit me together in my mother's womb. How precious*

are your thoughts about me, O God. They cannot be
numbered! –Psalm 139: 13-17 NLT

I cannot imagine a more beautiful and powerful message. God, the source of all, creates and says, "It is good." For me, this affirms that each human is of sacred worth—each human, a masterpiece of the Divine.

The act of throwing away was carried out.

***

Ben in family christening gown.
Photo by Olan Mills

We had carried our infant Ben to the front of our church congregation for baptism where the family of God promised to nurture and care for him and teach him the way of Jesus. This was a promise, a covenant and one that we believed to be sacred. We intended to ground him in love and care as we had been grounded to a commitment of love. This love took us to prison ministries, to another country and to shelters. This love prompted a young Ben to campaign for blankets to carry to children in orphanages and to want no harm to any living creature. The way of Christ did not include shaming of the authentic or condemning another human as unworthy . . . belittled and cast away. We were taught about the Good Samaritan who gave of himself to care for and ease the suffering stranger who represented an opposing people. Jesus taught that we see the value in all. We love by looking into the eyes of another as if that person were an angel in disguise. Ben was taught to look into the eyes of one who makes us feel uncomfortable as if we're peering into the eyes of Jesus.

All that Ben had been taught . . . was not available to *him* as an individual! What a betrayal, hypocrisy and lie . . . and all in the name of God!

***

Church leadership "talked to the youth leader." He continued as youth leader for a couple more years until voluntarily going to another church. The kind senior pastor is a person whom I do not believe could ever intentionally harm a soul. But he too was confused. Why wouldn't there be confusion when the Bible demonstrates a way of agape love, loving our neighbor and not judging? Yet there is a denominational *Book of Discipline* that states "the practice of homosexuality is incompatible with Christian teaching."

How dare they!

There were a few follow-up meetings. One was held at my work office. The youth leader, pastor and I met. I was told by the senior pastor that the two of them were sorry. The youth leader sat mostly without talking. Finally, I said to the youth leader, "You should be apologizing to *Ben*." However, in my heart, I was not going to put Ben in a position of sitting with this man who had traumatized him. We agreed that the youth leader would write Ben a thorough letter of apology.

Later, at home, I recapped the meeting for Ben. I told him to expect a letter. Weeks to months passed. No letter. I asked the pastor twice where the letter was. He seemed surprised that Ben had received no communication. Finally, a note was given to my friend Casey to give to us! When I gave the card to Ben, he opened the card and then threw it down on the table. On the front of the card was a gliding eagle with the words:

He Shall Mount Up with Wings as Eagles
Inside was handwritten:
Have a good school year.
It was signed with the youth leader's first name.

CHAPTER TWENTY-FIVE
FINALLY SPOKEN

When Ben was a senior in high school, I noticed he was talking quite a bit on the phone to someone. He frequently burst out laughing! I could hear him even though the door to his room was shut. He seemed so happy! He and his friend went to movies and went shopping together. Once they made vegan cupcakes at the friend's house.

One day Ben asked, "Can Robert spend the night on Saturday? We are working on a project for school and thought we would get it done this weekend."

Throughout Ben's life, from early years, I had sensed that he was gay. I loved the total package of Ben. If that were the case, I certainly never wanted to change him. I worried only about how others would treat him.

As I considered his request, I thought, Well, I really need to know. I asked, "Ben, if you are gay, can you tell me? I need to give you support whether straight or gay and to do that well, I need to know."

His reply was, "Well, I guess I am."

This is when and how the words were finally spoken. I shared my thoughts, "I want you to continue getting to know each other, but I just don't think that he should spend the night."

Ben accepted my decision.

About a month or two after that, Ben said, "Robert 'came out' to his parents. They immediately took him to see their pastor."

The pastor responded by asking, "Robert, do you believe in God and that Jesus is God's son?"

Robert answered, "Yes."

Ben reported to me that the pastor said, "Then it is not possible. It just can't happen. It's not possible for you, a male, to believe in Jesus and be attracted to a male. You must not really believe!"

Ben said, "He is so hurt. His parents said that he cannot live there if he is gay."

I asked, "Does he need a place to stay?"

Ben said, "He is okay for now, but he has to pretend that he is not who he is."

When I was in college in the eighties, I remember a panel that presented to our social work class. Each member of the panel was LGBTQ+. All shared their stories. I noticed one male classmate sitting with his arms crossed. Finally, when it was time for questions, he said, "It's just not natural."

One of the panelists so gently and respectfully provided a perspective, which really helped develop some of my thoughts around sexuality. He asked the classmate, "Are you attracted, physically and emotionally, to girls?"

The classmate abruptly responded, "Of course."

The panelist said, "Do you feel like it is just part of your make up, who you are?"

"Yes," the classmate said.

"What if I told you it is wrong for you to like girls. You must not, and furthermore, you must like men. Imagine what thoughts you would have and how you would feel? Son, it is no different for me. For me, it is not natural for me to be attracted to a woman. That, for me, would not be natural. I am who I am and just want to live my life."

The classmate continued in his discomfort, but I hope he thought about what the panelist explained.

Now I know we do not just fit into neat boxes, such as some are bi, some are fluid . . . but the point is, all have to live the life of their best authentic selves. All have a responsibility to discover, honor and claim each one's personal expression of humanity. Each has been molded and formed into uniqueness and with amazing gifts.

The subject of gender identity and sexuality falls into a spectrum of expression. Research is in process to validate whether DNA changes vary between gay individuals and heterosexual individuals. Research is in progress to validate if there are significant similarities in brain anatomy between gay persons and persons of the opposite sex. There is also a finding of crowding in some animal species being associated with homosexuality, but no research as yet determines whether this is applicable to humans.

A month went by. I noticed that Ben did not seem himself. It was as if a dark cloud had engulfed him. I asked, "Honey, what in the world is the matter?"

He said, "He doesn't love me anymore. He broke up with me." He sat beside me on the sofa with his head on my shoulder and sobbed.

I am so thankful that Ben let me in to what was happening. I am so thankful that I got to hold him. His teenage heart was broken. This was his first and the only relationship I know of him having. He later joked with his friends, "I may never have a long-term relationship; I'm just too picky."

Ben at age 16, at family reunion in Pipestem State Park, West Virginia.

Photo courtesy of Susan Hilliard.

Chapter Twenty-Six

DECISIONS

Once we had experienced a church locked in immobility, and much to my disbelief, we realized that good—through understanding, growth or justice—was not going to come out of the youth room experience, we left our beloved church with ease. We did not want any part of an organization that would not fight the harmful messages being sent by a youth leader. Even though some individuals did not agree with what had happened to Ben, the decisions made implied a shift in cultural norm regarding judgment and ranking of humanness. Many individuals were supportive but didn't know just *what* to do.

We stayed away from any church from 2008 until 2013. In my mind, I remained spiritual, but the church represented betrayal and toxicity.

But something happened in January of 2013. I wanted to go back. The youth leader had moved on several years before and there was a new pastor who had written some very inspirational newsletter messages challenging racism. Bill reached out to him and said, "Yes, beautiful message, but do you know what happened to a young gay kid at that church?

Bill was adamant that he did not want to go back and, in doing so, send a message to Ben, now a junior in college, that what happened to him was all right.

My argument for going was, "Ben doesn't want us to lose a part of our lives something that is meaningful, supportive and something that we missed. He should not be responsible for that."

I decided to visit. I went by myself. Some dear old friends who left when we did, also decided to come back for a visit on that same day. In front of me were friends, behind me and beside me. I took it as a sign that I should come back. Some commented, "It's awful what happened to dear Ben. I am so sorry." One said, "We did not know just what to do, Julie." Others looked at me and seemed to do back flips trying not to talk to me. Nevertheless, I decided to give it a try.

I talked to Ben on the phone while he was in college. I explained my rationale for going back and asked how he felt about it.

He said, "I want you to do what is best for you."

I felt he was sincere.

Ben, taking in the view.
Photo courtest of Ale Browning, a college friend.

Gradually, Bill and the girls visited the church with me. Even though some elements of being back felt like home, it also felt like there was a secret that was not being acknowledged. Dysfunctional. Each of us definitely experienced an internal conflict. The girls knew only that someone had been unkind to Ben. Although the person was no longer there, they really did not want to attend. The structure had become unfamiliar to them.

However, the people of the church showered us with support and kindness when Ben died. We continued to be involved for a short period of time, but we found it was just too painful to remain in that community.

It would be just months later we learned that the same time we started going back to church is when Ben stopped going to his college classes in January of 2013. January 29 was his last day. He faked his attendance with his friends but sat alone in a dorm room during class time. He met up with friends for dinner. While I wonder if Bill had been right about sending him a message that what happened was all okay, I also have to recognize that the information of the time was that it seemed like the right thing to do. If I led us down a wrong path, it was surely not intentional. All we can do is our best with the million decisions that we make each day. I realize that my return to church alone would not have ended Ben's desire to continue in this life.

CHAPTER TWENTY-SEVEN
HIS BODY

I don't remember the ride to the funeral home. We wanted to be with his body before cremation. My friend Casey was picking up Mom from her Assisted Living residence. My sister, Susan, and the pastor were with Bill and me. Charles, my father-in-law; his girlfriend; Tiffany, Ben's best friend; and her father were there.

A staff member asked, "Are you the mother of that beautiful, beautiful boy?"

I nodded yes, but there were no words.

Our friend who worked there said, "I made sure that the people doing the autopsy really took care of him. He has a little scrape on his nose, but we have him ready. His hair is just not all the way dry. Would you like a lock of his hair?"

"No," I said in a soft and empty manner.

"How about his fingerprint?"

I shook my head no. I didn't agree to take anything because I knew nothing would make anything better.

We met with the funeral director to plan the service. I asked, "Can we tell people just to be kind to each other? Maybe something good could come from this." My words were added to the bulletin by the pastor.

William Benjamin Wood
"Ben"

A Mother's Challenge

*"Please help make something good come out of this.
Be kind! Be good to all God's people. God loves us.
All of us are God's creation. Every person is beautifully made by God.
Not one sparrow falls from the sky without God knowing it.
All of us matter to God!"*

Julie Wood
May 9, 2013

The service bulletin
for William Benjamin Wood.

123

We walked through an entranceway into a long, long room. At the end of the room was a table, kind of like a stretcher. I don't remember feeling my feet or walking; the table just came closer to me.

Lying on that table was my William Benjamin Wood. He was wearing a soft blue, patterned hospital gown with snaps along the sleeves. I saw scratches on his wrists, but all superficial. His hair fell back away from his face. His face did not have the scruff that I was used to. It was clean shaven. His face was so beautiful. Even though Jesus would have been a Middle Easterner with dark hair and complexion, I thought, *He looks like Jesus.*

I knew I had to hold him, but I didn't know quite how. His autopsied body had been cut apart and studied. I could not pull him to me and wrap my arms around him. I moved to the head of the stretcher and leaned over him with my arms covering his arms. I had to face the pain. I felt his damp hair on my chin and neck, and I rested on his arms. I tried to soak into my very cells every aspect of my beautiful boy.

I intuitively knew that I had to see.

My sister was beside me, and the pastor was answering questions that my mom was asking. "Why does it make that sound when I touch him?"

The pastor lifted up the blanket to show blue, air-filled packing material beside his body.

Bill's father cried as he was held up by his girlfriend. He awkwardly said to Ben, "You know how much I love you."

I stood up. I knew that I had to look. I had to see what the medical examiner had described to me. I unsnapped the snaps on the arms of the gown. The upper, outer part of his left arm: slice, slice, slice, slice, slice. I instinctively placed my open hand on the cuts, yearning to erase, to heal the pain, the damage, the loss. My God, I would have done anything to mend the body and the spirit back to health and life. I used to place my hand on Ben's forehead as a child when he was falling asleep and pray that God would bless him and help me be what he needs me to be. I somehow felt that through my hand, I could send love right into his being. Now with my hand on him in surrender, I understood that my dear one was no longer here. My baby.

The second cut from the shoulder was the deepest . . . I wondered if this was the physical manifestation of the harm inflicted upon Ben by the man in the youth room who chose to stone a 16-year-old, kind and gentle soul. As I continued to look down the arm, the gown opened wider, exposing his chest with the raised Y of stitching. Susan said, "No, honey, that is from the autopsy," and she quickly pulled the covers up.

The other arm had no cuts. I held him again. I soaked him in. Nothing felt real—an observer and a broken mother, all at the same time.

Oh, my beautiful boy. He didn't tell me. He didn't call me.

***

Words as stones. Weapons of judgment, rejection, belittlement, shame and hate . . . a toxic waste bubbled up from that deep place screaming of endured cruelty—bearing witness to the injured soul. Life-stealing wounds as daggers ripped up and out through the flesh to make visible what had been stored in every cell of the body. Oppression paints an ugly, ugly truth! The canvas of Ben's life and body was striped in barbaric red lines!

As the mother of Emmett Till—the brutally beaten and killed 14-year old African-American young man—said in 1955, "I will make them see. You must look."

We may not turn our heads from the impact of belittlement, prejudice and harmful interpretation of theology.

***

It took months for the autopsy and toxicology reports to arrive. I read the description of each healthy organ, weighed and measured. There were no illegal drugs or alcohol in his system.

Several pain medications were present. They matched the postsurgical medications that I had been prescribed in 2012. I usually take as little medication as possible and thus the supply was almost full. I am sure that access to this gave Ben the way to end his suffering. This is an example of the importance of properly disposing of potentially deadly medications. Eliminating access to lethal means, in some cases, would at least make it more difficult to complete a plan for suicide. The cuts had no impact on ending his life. It was the medication that ensured the departure of one who decided living was just not worth the cost and pain.

Ben on UNCA campus.

Photo courtesy of Kim Labambard.

I wonder, but will never fully know when the voices of love were overpowered by the voices of shame and rejection. I will never know when

127

the balance tipped from a feeling of overall safety to one of fear. I do know that it happened. Ben, whose moral compass would not allow him to bring harm to even an ant, was in so much pain that he took action to end his own universe. Once he said, "Mom, isn't it amazing that in every 'body' is an entire universe of life?"

CHAPTER TWENTY-EIGHT

THE DORM ROOM

It was time to clean Ben's dorm room. Susan, my friend Casey, my niece and nephew, and Bill and I went to Asheville. Arrangements had been made with the Vice Chancellor to meet near the campus entrance and follow him to the dorm. Of course, none of this felt real. During the almost two-hour-and-thirty-minute drive, I imagined what may have played out on the early morning of May 8 . . . the suffering. I imagined the resident assistant walking into the room. How horrific the scene must have been! I felt so sorry for his pain.

As we approached Asheville, and the mountains were in view, the sky was beautifully blue and the clouds were puffy. The clouds seemed to spell B E N, at least that is the way I saw it. I remembered dropping Ben off on his first day of freshman year. I remembered the way he waved goodbye. He had plans to meet up with new friends whom he had made on-line; therefore, he was ready for us to leave much faster than we were ready to leave him. *Breathe, Julie, just breathe.*

Bill's head hung down. He was awake but not present . . . in emotional agony.

Traveling west, I thought about the many times Ben had traveled this highway. I looked over at the eastbound lanes. I imagined his drive one particular night: Cupid, Ben's dog, was then old and feeble. She began to fail fast and was confused. We had taken her to the vet but understood that her time to go was approaching.

Bill said sadly, "Let's wait. Ben will be home next week."

The situation moved from, "It is coming," to "She is now suffering." Cupid seemed to have developed dementia or some sort of cognitive and loss. She was lost. One night she got back behind the commode and was stuck. She was pitiful. We were all very sad.

Before going to bed, I called Ben at college and said, "Honey, we just cannot let Cupid suffer. We want to wait on you, but she is so much worse. It is time. It would just not be fair for her to have to wait. I'm sorry. We are going to have to take her to the vet to put her down tomorrow."

Ben said, "It is the right thing to do. I understand. I do not want her to suffer."

We fixed Cupid a space in the downstairs apartment kitchen where we could close the doors, making the space safe and simple. We fixed Cupid's bed, special food and water. When Bill and I went to bed, we set our alarm to go check on her and take her outside. Somewhere around 2 or 3 a.m., the alarm woke us and we went downstairs. There, sitting crossed legged in the middle of the kitchen floor, Ben was swaying back and forth, rocking his friend of thirteen years. His eyes were red.

The next morning, Sophie wanted to be present; Lacy did not. Ben, Bill, Sophie and I all had our hands on Cupid as she gently drifted away.

Ben with Cupid and some of his treasured stuffed animals.

***

At the college, we were greeted by the Vice Chancellor and the campus police chief. Each showed great compassion. They walked us to the tiny campus apartment. Bill did not really interact but moved with us. The shared apartment space was very small. There were four tiny bedrooms. One of the men put a key in the door to Ben's room and unlocked it. "Ma'am, we threw the sheets away and cleaned up the best we could."

I said, "Thank you."

Bill dropped to the floor. He seemed to be searching frantically for something. I looked around, looked at the poster on the wall, the pictures of family, Ben's books and at the floor. Apparently, Ben began the initial steps to take his life while in the raised loft bed. He must have fallen from there because his nose was scraped. I became aware of high-pitched whimpering echoing from the top of my throat. Deafening quiet separated the sounds of unfathomable sorrow. I had never made that sound before or after.

I heard Casey say, "Let's step out. She needs to cry. I have not heard her cry once."

I was too broken even to cry. I wish that I had screamed, yelled, shouted and blamed, but I just could not.

It is here in this place that brokenness cut life from a healthy young body, son, brother, cousin, friend, nephew and grandson.

With relief, Bill shouted, "I found it!"

It was Squishy Puppy. We believe now that Ben brought the stuffed beanie baby back to school to be found. There were also his favorite books, some of which he had asked me to read, but I had not. One was the *Wormwood Bible*. He would have known that these were important to us. He had also made mention to me several times that the band Radiohead was his favorite. There was a huge Radiohead poster on the wall.

I wondered if there was a message from the poster. I looked up Radiohead and immediately found the song titled "Creep." Yes, a message was left for us. These are some of the words:

When you were here before,
Couldn't look you in the eyes
You're just like an angel,
your skin makes me cry
You float like a feather
In a beautiful world
I wish I was special
You're so fuckin' special

But I'm a creep,
I'm a weirdo

What the hell am I doin' here?
I don't belong here

I don't care if it hurts,
I wanna have control
I want a perfect body
I want a perfect soul
I want you to notice
when I'm not around
You're so fuckin' special
I wish I was special . . .

We gathered his belongings and carried them home—family and friend's pictures, the Radiohead poster, the High School Reflections award certificate, dirty clothes, a coffee pot, cup, detergent and his old car covered in bumper stickers. That was all. A life had been lived and this along with his ashes became the remains.

***

Prior to his first breath, while in the womb, Ben had struggled between life and death. I was there. In his 21-year life, he experienced as much love as one could imagine, and he experienced as much rejection as one can imagine. I and others were there, suffered with him and attempted to remove the harmful messages to the best of our ability while we cherished and honored him.

Here again, this time within a tiny dorm room, he struggled between life and death, yet I was not there. He did not tell me. I did not feel it. I did not know. Alone in this space, hope was gone, action was taken to relieve himself of pain overtime. Here, where I stood, in one last breath, my child's life and soul left us.

The computer, phone and IPod had been wiped clean . . . as if he wanted to make his life disappear. Diminished and devalued. Gone. We loaded up, looked at the room and said goodbye. I said to the Vice Chancellor, "I'm very sorry that this has happened in this new dorm."

He said, "More students will come. They will not know." Later, I imagined a young Ben and I emotionally cleaning the room with a soapy cloth.

We were taken to his car. It too seemed to have been wiped clean. There was only enough gas to get to the station. We did find a Goodwill receipt under the seat. I guess that is where all of his belongings from home went.

The Vice Chancellor had arranged for us to spend time with his closest friends. We were hopeful that they could help us understand what had happened. Was there a breakup? No. They were devastated and absolutely filled with love. They knew that he had been sad but had no idea that his life was in danger. There was so much love among these friends. This is when we learned that he had not been going to class. The friends said that he had been put on academic probation. Ben? Ben loved school and learning. We had no idea.

In the quiet of the ride home, I remember the last end of the 2012 school year. There had been a surge of activity, debates, cruel conversations, robo calls and rallies in opposition to House Bill Amendment One, which targeted the removal of rights to those who are homosexual. Bill and I took part in rallies in protest of the Bill. The Amendment was filled with messages of devaluation and prejudice, and the sadness and threat hovered overhead like a dark cloud.

The day after Ben returned home for the summer, my birthday, the family attended a community event in a small, neighboring North Carolina town. Ben and I stood together in an open area. Bill had taken the girls to enjoy a ride while Ben and I watched and waited. The area was bustling with people in little family units. Many traditional couples held the hands of their young children and pushed baby strollers. We watched.

With a flat voice, Ben said, "Mom, I will never be accepted here."

"Oh, honey, most people are good and kind. They really are." I believed this and still do with all of my heart.

"Mom, you live in a bubble. You just don't know. It's the kind of work you do and the kind of friends you have. You do not see."

I did not see at the time that he was empty, angry and in the dangerous process of giving up . . . fueled by the insidious, heaping nature of repeated degrading harm.

"Honey, we just have to keep being a part of the teaching and the kindness. You will see. We have to believe. There is more goodness than meanness. I promise, Ben. I am very proud of who you are. Your beautiful heart and wisdom shine so brightly."

A few days later, on May 8, 2012, the state layered more harm by passing a bill of oppression.

We continued east on I-40. I, a social worker, missed the life-threatening signs of one giving up hope. Ben took his life on the one-year anniversary of Amendment One.

This bill was ruled unconstitutional in October 2014. Every act and decision has a ripple effect on the lives of others. I wonder the cumulative harm to gay or straight this government-sanctioned public shaming and rejection caused in its short-lived existence. Always, the oppressed is left injured as well as the oppressor.

CHAPTER TWENTY-NINE

TIME TO RETURN TO WORK

When it was time to return to work as a program manager in a human services agency, I found the process very robotic. It felt surreal packing my lunch and dressing for a new life of "after." The last time I sat in my office chair was before Ben died. I developed a daily pattern of getting in the car and sobbing. I was alone; it was private; and I was free to allow the pain to swallow me up. Developing ownership of the reality of the after seemed to be a carving process. So much cutting away and so much reforming—pain overtime. I regularly arrived at work with swollen eyes, streaked make-up and a red face. But oh, how beautiful the care was!

On my first day, I approached my office door, reached in my bag to secretly grasp Ben's favorite tie-dye tee shirt that I had tucked inside and unlocked the door. All felt so strange because birthday confetti was still stuck to the carpet, and cards for my 50th were scattered about. A picture of my three kids was on the wall. It was evidence of the life before. Standing inside the door, I wondered, *Who am I now? The person who left here can never return. She is now gone.*

Ben, Lacy and Sophie at Salem Lake, 2010,
the photo on display in the author's office.
Photo courtesy of Susan Hilliard.

The team always greeted me, showing so much love. They checked in with me, made a sign for my door for when I needed to be alone, held me and said my child's name. They knew him and they supported me. At times, I felt as I focused on the needs of the day as if my spirit and soul had a respite. Yet, I was safely allowed to move with the waves of grief as they came, small or large. It was with sacred respect that I always see this love. Yet, while my experience was just what I needed, I have been shown that each grieving individual needs different acts of love. My husband worked with caring people too. They respected and were dedicated to him. They were willing to support him through recovery as much as possible. He tried to fulfill the duties of his position yet was struggling, barely limping along. They felt that to "talk about it" would make it unbearably hard. In an attempt to protect, a "hush order" was sent out before my husband returned to work saying, "Do not talk about it." Bill was heartbroken. He felt misunderstood, uncared for and invalidated.

I thought, *Wow. How heartless! Bill felt dishonored and abandoned.*

During the same time period, a peer, working in another part of the state but with my same company, lost her daughter to cancer. I called her to say I understood and asked, "How are you?"

Her explanation surprised me and presented me another pebble of insight. She said, "Julie, I do all that I can to get out of bed, dress and drive to work. I just pray that no one will say anything about my daughter. I do not want compassionate faces, touches on the shoulder or other acts of kindness." She said, "I make it in the door and someone is sure to say, 'How are you. I am so sorry.'"

My friend, crying, said, "How can they do that? Do they not know how very hard I am trying to hold myself together? They bring my dear daughter up, the tears begin to flow, and I cannot even function. All that I can do at that point is leave and go home. Do they have no heart at all?"

I told her then about Bill's pain in an almost opposite situation.

Witnessing these three scenarios, I have come to realize that many people want to help those in grief. But, my goodness, how does anyone know what to do or say? What I believe is a good takeaway in understanding is that friends, coworkers, family may ask, "How may I be the most supportive?" Support persons cannot assume what is most supportive for an individual's pain. And those who grieve need to be open and honest to say, "For me, I would like to ask that you say his name . . . validate my feelings . . . do not bring it up . . . give me a break by letting life be normal for a bit of time." All of this requires courageous trust and tender love.

CHAPTER THIRTY
NO ONE TO RESCUE

I was now aware of the magnitude of Ben's suffering. Before he left us, I did not know. In the aftermath, an urgent feeling to rescue; to pour my love and strength into him; and to hold him physically, emotionally and spiritually stirred in my being, creating a constant flow of adrenaline. It took time to recognize it. I could see myself drying tears, making a step-by-step action plan and narrating a message to give light. I wish I could have given Ben hope—slipping in between the darkness, as light slipped between the tree's leaves—to proclaim it will get better. Wow, I would have given anything to ease his pain. Also true, for me, I needed to protect and nurture him. I needed to relieve my pain by making it better . . . meeting the needs of my child. Maybe the need is rooted in a deep-seated desire to have some control and influence. Maybe, psychologically, we are driven to action to lessen our own helplessness. Still, driven by love, I would have given all of myself to ease his suffering.

One day, an awareness came that began soothing the adrenaline flow. I realized my need to respond was *my* need now and not a need for relief of Ben's pain. Ben did not need my response nor could I help. He was away from hate and had to endure no more misdirected insecurity and anger on this earth. Ben was wrapped in the safe arms of love.

Ben at Hanging Rock.
Photo courtesy of Evelyn Pierce.

Growing in my thoughts was a feeling for the many who sit as a target in the circle of rejection and judgment. The church and society that I am a part of must heal and mature to find justice, honor and love as grounding principles in which to exist.

I can imagine Jesus soaking in the pain of others, observing the unjust practices and feeling overwhelming human helplessness. He must too have felt the deep longing to bring comfort and to soothe and counsel in order to ease the suffering in the lives of those around him. A rescue. Blessed are the depressed, those who grieve, those who are meek—meaning controlled or oppressed— and those who are hungry and thirsty. When men reproach and persecute for righteousness sake— wow . . . the persecuted will be blessed! For the Bible follower, beautiful lessons such as these must be celebrated as a gift in guiding us. The message is given with clarity, and we must recognize the flaw in the injustice that is occurring when humans attempt to determine favor or worthiness! The cost to all is devastating. It ripples out to our families, society, country and world. But oh how the ripple that comes from compassion, gentleness, kindness and empowerment also expands with a strength to heal this earth and those who reside on it.

Blessed are the merciful, pure-hearted (not egocentric) and the peacemaker. The way of love, how to be with one another, has been explained. Has the message been distorted by the dark side of the human condition while sheltered in obedience? Is it possible for the struggle to have been fed by fear and the ego individually and collectively? Am I, are we, mature enough to look within our individual and collective souls to figure out this truth so we may all be free? Maybe, the individual and collective conscious was blind to the imposition of so much harm! Once we see though, we cannot unsee. And once we see, we must embody healing change as an instrument for and thus as a receiver of peace, joy and love.

As we develop, I believe, the world would change with a commitment to do no harm and for us as its people to mature to capacity and willingness to agree to disagree. Eventually it is possible to respect the other, the wisdom of the truth in each, the interpretations and understandings, providing space for each to enter a place of individual calling—the claiming of authenticity. May people accept in peace and moral conviction that each has a relationship between themselves and God. One person must not inflict his or her own will on what binds another in relationship with God.

CHAPTER THIRTY-ONE
GRAY TO COLOR

The world turned gray in the depths of my grief. Nothing seemed special, beautiful, bright or colorful.

About four or five months after Ben's death, Bill and I planned a weekend getaway to the mountains of North Carolina. We stayed in a beautiful bed and breakfast with a huge rocking chair porch and view of the mountains. Tearful moments crept in. We felt that we needed to share with the host couple that we had recently lost our son. They gave us a book about grief as a gift.

We awkwardly functioned in a cloud of loss. I spent time sitting by a little stream, under the trees, still trying to metabolize this new existence. While there, I looked for stones that felt special, but there were none. I was aware of the sound of the water, the presence of the ferns, the large size of the rhododendron and the smell of the woods, but I just could not care. I could not make myself feel the feelings that I had enjoyed throughout my life. I did not care.

On Saturday we strolled through antique shops and discovered a farmer's market in my birth town of Burnsville. Although we used to love quick trips to the mountains, we didn't talk much. We just went through the motions. It was all okay, just sort of, well . . . gray.

It was Sunday morning, and we would be leaving soon. I woke up early and Bill continued to sleep. In a little sitting room connected to the bedroom was a window seat. I sat and looked out at the mountain range. I noticed that this house was positioned perfectly to see through a gap between two close-up hills, to a range of blue mountains. The opening between the hills reminded me of a view finder. I opened the window, listened to the birds and watched a hawk glide, tilting his wings to create a slow and peaceful circle. I even pulled out my phone to record the hawk and the singing of the birds. For about twenty minutes, I found peace.

I sat back from the window seat and became aware of a flower box hanging from the window. It had been there the entire time but just grabbed my attention now. The flowers were absolutely beautiful with lots of purple, blue, red and yellow with varying shades and shapes of green leaves.

In this moment, I recognized that I was seeing and appreciating color and beauty for the first time in months. God . . . in every blossom, in the dirt and in the moisture beaded on each leaf.

Butterfly in glorious color.
Photo courtesy of Susan Hilliard.

CHAPTER THIRTY-TWO

TOTAL DISREGARD

I had an experience that provided me with much greater insights into the journey of the oppressed. Most of my life has been lived in a privilege that I didn't even know that I had. In June 2015, two years after Ben's death, I was involved in a church conference-wide vote regarding removing hurtful language from the United Methodist, *Book of Discipline*. Me, a straight, white, middle-aged daughter of a United Methodist pastor, was given the experience of being victim of insidious harm. It is the kind of harm that is heaped upon previous harm with a multiplying impact. I had absorbed harm caused through prejudice: the mistreatment of LGBTQ persons by the Church.

The group was instructed to vote by standing. First, the vote to remove the hurtful language. Otherwise, the *Book of Discipline* would say "The practice of homosexuality is incompatible with Christian teaching." I stood. It was beautiful to see so many people rise up. Hum . . . people were still sitting though. Then it was time for the vote indicating a desire to keep the derogatory language. With the sound that I know from movie theater seats, chairs begin to flip up as people stood. The sound echoed across the large auditorium with about 1,200-1,500 people. My head fell down into my hands. How do they not see what they are doing? They don't understand? My mind was racing, my body queasy and on fire. Panic filled me. I held screams inside. I felt as though my insides were quivering. My body began to shake.

With the power and impact of an assault, a man behind me triumphantly shouted "God is Good!"

With my mouth contorted, trying to control the crying, I turned around to the man behind me. "How? How can you believe this way? People are suffering and dying because of these words, this dogma. My son. My son is dead! He is dead! These words took the life of my son."

His response was, "Lady, the church didn't do anything to your boy."

I looked into his narrowed and fixed eyes. I recognized the clinched jaw. I had seen this adamant righteousness before. This was a different face but with the same look and tone. Then I felt myself lose my grounding. His attachment to judgment completely blinded him to my pain.

He felt no compassion for me or Ben. He did not soften to show mercy. His ego would not allow him to see or feel my plea. Dismissed, I was completely overwhelmed with panic. *Why can't they understand? Why don't they care?* Echoes of the flipping sound continued in my sleep. The use of God to justify hate . . . flip . . . flip . . . flip . . .

After conference, the tears did not stop. My outlook and my attitude seemed to be shifting to the cup half-empty instead of half-full. I was increasingly sad and so very tired. *Why are people so mean-hearted?* Everywhere I looked, things appeared cruel, and I started to accept that no, the Church will never care to understand. There will be more kids, more people. They will be betrayed, rejected and shamed. There is no one who will hear our voice. No wonder Ben gave up! Insidious harm continued, subtle, but potentially with fatal consequences. There was a fading of life. It was much like when water spills on a watercolor painting. The water seeps and spreads out slowly to diminish the color and the light and to distort life.

I recognized that I needed help to understand what was happening to me. I sought the help of a therapist. He explained that trauma can get "stuck" in the brain. He used EMDR (Eye Movement Desensitization and Reprocessing) to help me process the trauma amplified by the vote. The sounds of the chairs stopped intruding upon my thoughts, and I came to recognize that "The Vote" was another enlightening part of my life journey.

The wounded tree in the mist reflects anguish..

Photo courtesy of Susan Hilliard.

Early in this experience, when exposed to one spewing condemnation, I typically felt a surge of rage. At the time, I felt right and justified to condemn right back. Eventually, I learned this power struggle brought no good fruit at all. After our family was deeply injured by the treatment and judgment of the God-given essence of Ben, I became afraid . . . quivering afraid. Post-Traumatic Stress afraid. I felt that these interactions were toe to toe with the devil himself. Panic has taken me over on several occasions. But as with everyone else on this planet, I have continued to discover, learn and grow. I want to boldly, peacefully and confidently speak love, claiming my space and my value. This is what I pray to develop.

CHAPTER THIRTY-THREE

I SEE

Sometimes we really don't see until we see. When we see, our awareness changes, and a shift in our understanding occurs. For example, in the medical field, there are best practices. The best practices of even ten years ago are quickly superseded according to the latest information. Understandings and beliefs change. Sometimes we don't take the time to notice until someone we love is negatively impacted. Some things come hard and some things come naturally.

I know that there are many good and kind people of faith who have not been exposed to the harm that has been caused by the beliefs around sexuality. They believe they are obeying God-inspired Scripture and following tradition. I imagine we must have a filter so that much of what we interpret as right is influenced by our relationship with authority. Some people as children may have been given grounding parameters and the tools to assess and seek through real self-examination, meditation and prayer. We are all a hodge-podge of inherent and formed strengths and weaknesses; at times we get it right and at times we get it wrong.

Amazing array of trees, blue sky and white clouds.
Photo courtesy of Susan Hilliard.

I have been a participant in making a misstep with the potential of causing harm. I still feel sick on my stomach when I think of something I once said as a youth to someone. I called someone—not with Down Syndrome or from Mongolia—a mongoloid boy. This was a term inappropriately used at that time for an individual with Down

Syndrome. I am so ashamed that I said something so insensitive. I can't even imagine what my intent was. But I find it interesting that I have since worked with people with intellectual disabilities for my entire career. I strongly believe that some of the wisest people whom I have ever known have had some of the lowest IQs. I have been a strong advocate for the rights of people with disabilities and a problem solver on their behalf. Maybe my horrid mistake was used for good in shaping me into who I am. I share in the human journey of figuring out what is real. I am no better, no worse, but I must try to use my life for good.

Others, including Maya Angelou, teach us that we stand upon the shoulders of those who have come before in strength, knowledge and courage. They are with us. We must consider that we are also impacted by those who come before us bearing fear, bias and any belief system that orders and ranks worthiness with a practice of rejection of persons different than oneself.

Even though that youth leader is responsible for his choices, we may even consider that the words, expression and taunts were not his alone. These words, as in his case, may be a spoken reflection of fear from threatened egos passed through generations, showing up through expectations, scornful looks and policies. These policies include those addressing homosexuality in *The Book of Discipline* in one denomination or in votes by governments—all of which set the stage for cultural norms within the associated group. I do not believe the youth leader arrived on the scene alone.

I do believe that somewhere along the way he accepted and then delivered the message that persons who are gay are inferior and threatening. His rightness was so strong for him that he was able to justify degrading a child. There are no words from Jesus rejecting those who love another of the same sex nor a mention even back to the ten commandments. In fact, David, described in both the old and new testaments (1 Samuel 13:14; Acts 13:22) as a "A man after God's own heart," said of his friend Jonathan:

> I am distressed for thee, my brother Jonathan: very pleasant hast thou been unto me: thy love to me was wonderful, passing the love of women. 2 Samuel 1:26 KJV.

It seems that something with such condemnation would at least have to have been in the top ten or spoken by Jesus. Yet, some feel they must treat such individuals as second class, or even worse, cast them away. I have, however, read and heard, loudly and clearly, from Jesus a prominent theme of love with the greatest expectation to love God and love one another. We are to be hospitable, welcoming, merciful . . . let the little children come to me . . . do not push any aside.

After Ben died, I thought a lot about how behavior is shaped by words in policies. Of course, that is why policies exist. Guidelines and policies are most certainly developed to be the basis for decision making, to make clear and to direct. It is this framework that forms cultural norms with potentially far-reaching implications.

Anti-discrimination laws are enacted to protect individuals from unfair treatment based on each person's God-given traits, especially those that are in conflict with existing rules that allow for unjust discrimination upon certain groups rather than to comfort persons yearning to feel acceptable and worthy.

We must fully accept that we are already loved. Those who are guided by biblical writing believe each has been woven together and is known by God before ever born. Each is God's child who is good. Each soul is brought into this life acceptable, worthy, special and with the right to be and live authentically. This honors God. Too frequently, contradictory messages within laws, policies and books of discipline create confusion. How would there not be paralysis when one seeks guidance only to find polarizing directives?

I wonder if people in the past and in the present have managed the contradictory messages with avoidance. For example, kindhearted persons of faith who earnestly believe that God's perfect plan is for a man and woman to become "one flesh" and that same gender sexual partnerships are wrong, may have looked away, failing to dig deeper to discern and seek understanding. Within that framework, they may or may not have considered the examples of God's love and treasure of individuals who have acted outside of God's ideal will. Nor have they taken action that would reject or inflict harm to a gay person . . . they looked away.

In another example, some kindhearted persons, who earnestly believe that love is about emotional, spiritual and intimate attraction and do not feel in judgment of same sex partnerships, may also have looked away when the church or others used exclusionary language that has at times caused significant harm to gay persons. They too fail to dig deeper to discern and seek justice.

All of this avoidance has contributed to tension building to crisis. Maybe all will grow to an understanding that it is not ours to condone or to judge. Of course, in abuse or victimization we must help and seek just practice and care. Each must seek and honor God's will in one's own life as a reflection of God. One cannot feel the will of God for another. Each person is cherished with God's unlimited mercy abounding . . . the plan that brings good fruit. We must not—any of us— condone or tolerate infliction of spiritual trauma. That is incompatible with Christian teaching!

***

There are those who see religion adapting with societal changes, but keeping a message of love. For example, most religions do not accept that a man, husband, father can treat another, such as a woman or child, as property. Most religions do not accept slavery of any human, the physical stoning of female adulterers, casting away those who are divorced or a requirement of beards of a certain length. Many do not believe that only heterosexual men are called to ministry by God.

We wanted change to happen. If Ben had to die, how could his death be used to help others see the harm being done and prevent another from being treated in a demeaning way—as an irritating nuisance?

We met with a church bishop. He shook his head and said, "I am so sorry." I have no doubt that he was being sincere. He followed with, "There is nothing I can do. I do not even get a vote."

Once love is put aside, everyone feels disempowered. Some even hang their heads with a sickening feeling in their hearts and stomachs, knowing that they are participating in something that is wrong by not doing something to change it, but feeling the man-made rules on the books must be followed. There is a toxic conflict internalized. The very basic ideas of religion are rooted in love. All the primary world religions have a foundational principle of the "Golden

Rule": to treat others, our neighbors, as we would like to be treated. This is so profound. God is love, mercy, compassion, forgiving and justice. There is a belief that in contrast, spiritual darkness kills, steals and destroys.

I believe with all I know, that when religion rejects people based simply on who they are, this is an act of extreme psychological violence. Darkness. When people justify shaming and rejection in the name of God, they have formed an image of a God that might as well be the "devil" to many victims and all who love them. No loving God would ever create individuals to suffer as a result of this divine masterpiece. Surely this is self-evident. This is the human condition. Humans fight their own insecurities at the cost of others who are also of sacred worth. I now understand John Wesley's statement—when talking to some who believed in a different theology—"Your god is my devil." Yes, this god who ranks people as worthy or unworthy based on their authentic identity is who I define as my devil!

CHAPTER THIRTY-FOUR
FORGIVENESS

When I think of the bullies Ben encountered, I do not have hate for them. I do have grief from and disbelief in their actions. I wonder how the idea that one is empowered and privileged to belittle and dominate another was formed in the bully.

I once heard Ben say, "So if someone thinks that being gay is wrong and that person is not gay, then let's acknowledge we disagree and move on. Why would that person even care about my choices if I am not hurting anyone? Why do they think who I love is their business? I don't know how they can be so passionate about something that does not affect them."

Ben is one of many who has experienced a diminished feeling of esteem, value and safety. The percentage of suicide attempts and completed among gay persons is four times more likely than heterosexual persons.[1] The chance of suicide increases dramatically with each traumatizing event.

Forgiving myself is a task as well as the process of forgiving others. I continuously remind myself that each is on a journey and each is learning and growing each day. Forgiving myself has been complex. The process of forgiveness needs to be reworked whenever I re-encounter a memory about something I missed.

One of the hardest is not having seen his room empty. I crumble with the question, *What if he wanted us to find it empty? What if I could have taken off for Asheville and scooped him up to safety? Was he shocked that we did not come to him?*

I must also recognize that it is possible that if we saw the empty room, were alarmed and approached him, he may have had a perfectly reasonable explanation to relieve our concern. He had been talking about wanting to stay in Asheville, getting a job and renting an apartment. He could have easily convinced us that he took his things in hope that the apartment plan was working out. He then may have completed his departure anyway. There is no way to know.

What if I had given more attention to his comments made at the festival of 2012 about not being accepted for being himself? I do know

---

1 The Trevor Project. http://www.thetrevorproject.org

that we talked about counseling. He convinced me that he really did not need or want to go. He always spoke with such wisdom. I had the opinion of Ben as rock-wise and strong . . . the one who rose above it all. He always shared openly with me and his friends. We did insist that he go to a therapist after the events in the youth room. He and the therapist felt he was processing as well as possible and had framed the experience in a healthy way.

Maybe Ben was just so smart that he knew how to mask his internal suffering by saying the right things. A couple of times, I talked with him about depression symptoms. I said, "Genetically, you have a slightly increased chance for depression and anxiety." We talked about signs and that support is there to help if ever needed. He was well educated and always reassured me that he understood and knew what to do. We had also participated in therapy when he was in elementary school because there was some indication that he was socially nervous . . . with good reason, given the experience of bullying. He did not grow up in an environment that presented mental health challenges as a weakness. I really believe that he understood the chemistry—no different than my thyroid condition, I used to say—of mental health issues.

It still hurts like a knife to my soul to think about what I missed. I have reasoned, *Well, if I was supposed to be aware, I would have been.* I can calm myself with the knowledge that I did much that was right. I would have done anything for him. I had no awareness that his room was empty or that he was in trouble. If it had entered my awareness, I would have given the depth of all that I am to provide more support and resources for my son.

Bill came a long way in his recovery, but the circumstances of Ben's pain and suicide created a loss to his well-being that was severe. His profession of more than thirty years was highly rewarding but also was one of high responsibility. Time proved that he was just unable to provide the level of expertise that he once did, and the level of stress was detrimental to him. Ben, Bill and I were changed forever by the church injury. Our grief was momentous and the harm real.

When Ben died, the change created many shattered pieces and layers of complications within our grief. Some of the shattered pieces could be used to produce new awareness, but for Bill, many pieces could not be put back together. In retirement, he began to find a new normal that included times of laughter, many home-cooked meals and a life simplified and good. He was always ready to jump and help his family. We, all who loved Ben, were picked up and placed on a different path than what we were on when Ben lived.

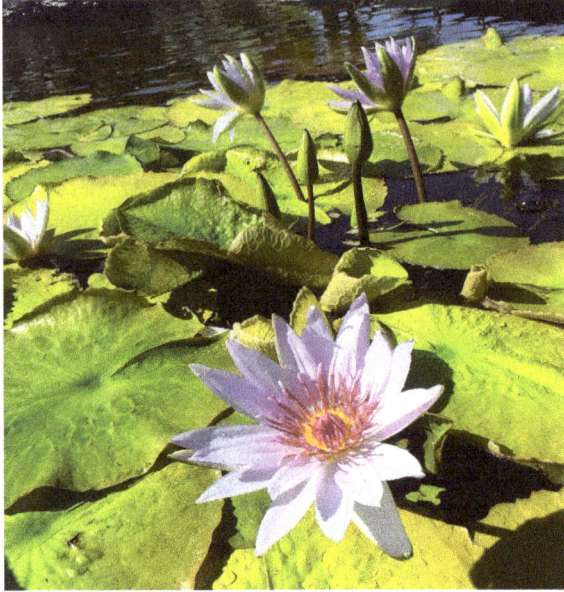

Water lilies.
Photo courtesy of Susan Hilliard.

Lacy and Sophie each found a way to process and express the loss of their brother.

Lacy found her outlet through dance. She wrote in a college application that she had struggled her entire life with expressing her feelings but found through movement that her feelings may be let out and shared. "This is how I learned who I am."

My Sophie, at 16, began the process of peeling back layers of emotion. She did a very brave thing. She said, "Mom, I don't want to hurt you, but you were not there for me when Ben died. I kept being sent away. I didn't understand what was happening, and I was told, 'Be good. Don't cause your parents any stress.'"

She said, "Everyone was centered around you and Dad, and we were pushed away to cause you less stress. Lacy and I were just so confused."

More than heartbreak, I felt great respect that she was able to speak the words. I knew that she had been angry with me but thought that it may just be part of a mama and daughter teen-years relationship. I am incredibly thankful that she shared such complicated and hard emotions. I was able to say, "You are right. I was not there. I could do nothing more than survive during those days."

She said, "I know. I know you did all that you could, but I was still in a house filled with many strangers, people coming in and out of my room, and I was just pushed out. I was so afraid. I was so afraid that I would throw up."

We cried. I thanked her for speaking her truth. It truly is another layer of the f____ horrible. Real, true, loving and vulnerable . . .

After this uncovering, of course many thoughts and emotions had to be processed. I deliberately had to focus my thoughts on not trying to justify, defend, or gloss over . . . no, this is real and true, and we all did the very best that we could. This is.

A month or so later, Sophie's sweet little cat, Tiger, who had rarely been out of the house, slipped out of our yard and crossed over the six-foot, privacy fence and into the yard of two, 10-month-old, huge, Great Dane puppies. Sophie was in her upstairs room, which was beside the yard with the Great Danes. She heard her little Tiger screaming.

She looked out and recognized the dainty, pink collar among the moving bodies. She screamed for Bill; they ran out but were unable to get through the fence that had been barricaded and tied to keep the mischievous and clever puppies in. Thank goodness, the owner drove in the driveway, went out and with difficulty got the dogs off Tiger. Bill went through the neighbor's house with a towel to wrap up the injured kitty. Tiger was dead.

I was leaving an event and checked my messages. There were calls and texts from Bill, "Come home now, please."

I quickly called. Bill said, "Sophie is completely broken. Tiger died."

I got home. As I approached our house, I saw a teal towel lying by the door, swaddling the little kitty. I picked it up and rubbed Tiger's sweet and always-so-soft little head. I always loved the way her tabby stripes made a pattern around her face and the top of her head.

I heard someone running down the inside steps and then heard the wail of my girl. I ran in and held her. She completely melted into my embrace. I said, "I'm so, so sorry, baby."

She cried, "I couldn't get in. I couldn't get through the gate. She was trying to get away, and they kept catching her. She was crying out."

"Oh, honey, I know that rips your heart out. I know how much you love Tiger and how you would protect her. I know this hurts so much."

"I tried to climb the fence."

We moved to the sofa where she laid her head in my arms. I kissed her head and stroked her hair and cheek. "Sometimes there is nothing that we can do," I said. "Of course, we love and would do anything that we could; but sometimes, darling, we just do not have that opportunity. Honey, you gave her so much love. That is what you did for her. Sometimes, we cannot make the world safe and fix all the bad things that happen. You are so full of love, Sophie, and love is powerful, but we cannot keep all that we love safe at all times. Our job is to love and care to the best of our ability."

My teenager, loving and strong, was able to allow me to hold, stroke and pour out my love . . . to hold her through pain. Sacred.

CHAPTER THIRTY-FIVE

HOPE THROUGH NEW MESSAGES

A few months after Ben died, we found Green Street United Methodist Church. It is a Reconciling Ministries congregation. This means that all are welcome. People are greeted by a diverse congregation that reflects the community in which it sits. The pastors' stoles are in rainbow colors. As Pastor Kelly says, "The church is made up of black, brown, white, gay, straight, upper class, middle and lower class and people with no class at all."

Being in this community is validating, comforting and healing. Home.

I have had the opportunity to get to know an amazing retired bishop of the United Methodist Church. He is from Tennessee and is an African-American pastor. He lived through the horrible years of the civil rights struggle and was even jailed with Dr. Martin Luther King. His story is amazing.

He fought long and hard for desegregation. He is an avid teacher and advocate for the dignity and honor of all God's children as he teaches biblical obedience. I love and admire him. Bishop Melvin Talbert once spoke at Green Street and said, "This church is an answer to many, many prayers. This is real."

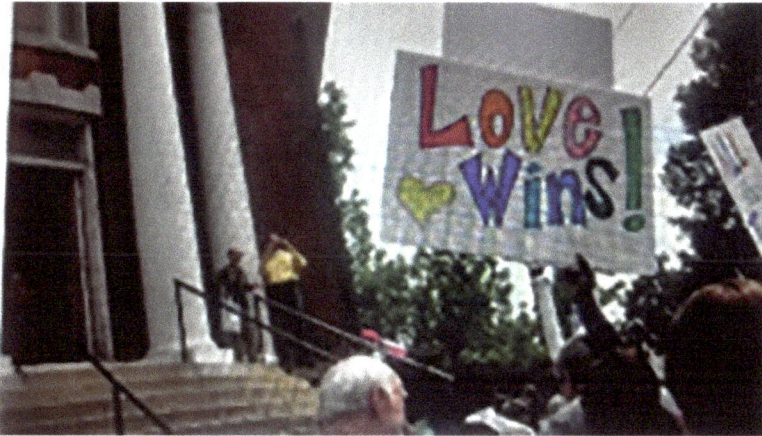

Green Street United Methodist Church.

Messages are powerful, so very powerful and delivered in so many ways. Although Ben's youth group experience was the most impactful event of harm heaped on him, I can't say that alone caused his death. We can acknowledge that he may have had a genetic predisposition for depression. We can acknowledge that he was a bullied child. We can accept that if we had seen his room, there is a possibility that the outcome would have been prevented. We can accept that if we had not gone back to that old church, he may have been at a different emotional place. We can acknowledge that if someone at the school, a professor perhaps, had reached out to Ben when he stopped attending class or if we had been notified, interventions may have been instituted. Even after keeping these in mind, I know with all that I am that if he had received the message from spiritual leaders, "You are a beautifully created child of God, who's authenticity is unique and a gift unto the world," he would have been strengthened in layers of protection that would have sustained him. He would not have died. If the old church had recognized and named the abuse that took place in the youth room and had taken responsibility for the misguided theology, he would not be dead. I just know.

Like the pastor of the old church said, "If I could go back and change what happened, I would." I believe him. I do not believe anyone would have chosen to contribute to the outcome that occurred. This just is.

***

I've learned that the loss of a child is a pain that changes throughout time. It is not something that one can just get over. A few years ago, during a time of self-examination, a concept developed that has proven a way to understand and describe my progression through the stages of grief.

The gut-punching sadness is never more than a thought away, and my loss circulates as blood through my body. Maybe it is like a conjoined twin . . . connected yet independent in identity. My grief does not have to consume me . . . be me. The love between a parent and a child does not require it, nor does it want it. I may continue to live my life in purpose, joy and peace while in relationship with the grief living beside me. I think that this is the best that it can be. I recognize the everlasting bond with my son that is in every heartbeat and breath. I am exceedingly grateful for my phenomenal teacher, Ben.

***

While giving a sermon in the fall of 2014, demonstrating a tremendous gift for words and the strength of great vulnerability, a divinity student courageously shared his journey of rejection and his excruciating loss of relationship and support from his close-knit family. This heartbreaking loss came after his family learned that he is gay. He shared in his sermon his grief, struggle, loss of hope and his gratitude for the faith that has sustained him. He referenced the death by suicide of a young college student by the name of Ben Wood. He did not know that I, the mother of Ben, was there in the congregation and a member of Green Street Church. The divinity student and I were both astonished when we were introduced by Pastor Kelly.

The young man was interning as the youth director, and our girls began attending the youth group. He was a wonderful and fun teacher. The girls loved him. Over time, we became more and more familiar with each other. It was a great honor when he offered Bill and me his family tickets to attend his graduation from graduate school.

With growing care and relationship, I felt that more needed to be stated: "You are not Ben, you are you. You can never—nor do we want you to—fill the hole left by his absence. Bill and I are not your parents and can never replace that loss, but we surely love you for who you are, and we are here for you."

"I'm here for you too," he said.

Initially we were drawn together by the "dark ugly" that had cost each of us so dearly. Respect, understanding, enjoyment and connection soon sealed a bond of love. Family.

It is humbling and amazing how God is always ready to bring about the unexpected. A rich and beautiful collateral blessing.

***

If we could check ourselves by evaluating what impact our actions have, we would see what is truly of God and what is not. Proactively, the disciples asked, "How will we recognize false prophets, Jesus? When you are not here, how will we know what is truly of God?"

Jesus' guidance was:

By your fruits you will know them. Matthew 7:15-20 RSV

Such a beautiful and powerful truth.

The bad fruit of racial segregation was recognized by the Methodist church in the early 70s after much sacrifice, education and advocacy in the 60s. The church became racially united, at least in discipline. Ironically, another group of people was identified for "segregation." The practice of homosexuality as incompatible with Christian teaching was written into *The United Methodist Book of Discipline*. The same discipline proclaimed the sacred worth of all. Hence, another cycle of collaborative confusion and paralysis. But *abuse* of an individual *because* he or she is a homosexual is incompatible with Christian teaching. The church must be a place of ensured safety and ensured celebration of God's beautifully diverse creation. Currently in 2020, while there are bumpy roads to come, plans are being made for the removal of the derogatory and exclusionary language, which may very possibly result in a division in the church.

***

I was recently asked, "What do you think Ben would like to say to us?"

I reflected on Ben always considering historical context. To my amazement, words came to mind after a full night's sleep. I simply wrote them down. I believe Ben's message would have been:

In the 1600s, in the name of God, people with birthmarks and moles might have been tried and convicted as a child of the devil or as a witch. My youngest sister, Sophie, was born with a hemangioma on her left cheek. It was bright red, raised and almost an inch in diameter. When she was born, it was in the shape of a heart. When I held her and her face rested on my face, the area felt extra warm. It was just a part of her. If she had been a baby of the 1600s, she might have suffered through fire, death by pressing torture or confinement. Humans proclaiming the will of God might have declared her an insult to God and a threat to society. I can imagine the piercing screams of agonizing pain. But no, Sophie is free to enjoy life, to feel the breeze on her cheek and through her hair as she rides along on her galloping beloved horse. She can soak in the sunset as she feeds her horse. Sophie intuitively provides courage and support to children and adults with disabilities and to animals of all kinds. Thank you, God, that eyes were opened. Sophie was born in 2003.

After the bombing of Pearl Harbor, Asian Americans were forced to live inside the fences surrounding internment camps. There was a prejudice born in fear. The belongings and rights were removed from these innocent Americans. Just think, what if my Asian-American sister was a child of the 40s? She might have stood with her fingers holding onto the metal patterns of the fence that holds one inside and separate as a castaway. Her eyes might have peered out to imagine scenes of the life that she was missing because she had been thrown away, deemed a threat to society. But no, Lacy is free to thrive, dance, inspire, laugh and teach! Thank you, God, that eyes were opened. Lacy was born in 2001.

We now look back and think, *How very foolish! How could they have reasoned in a way to draw such misguided conclusions? How frail can our tiny little human egos be?* I, the mother of Ben, must be his voice to tell his story. He was kind, funny, a dedicated learner, an advocate for equity and one sensitive to the needs of others whom he counseled with wisdom—a wise old soul. He would take an ant outside or capture a bee to release outside so that it could live. He gave value and honored the authentic truth that each person must find. He was a faithful and supportive friend, son, brother, grandson, nephew and even citizen. He had integrity and was a leader. He was an active member of the United Methodist church . . . until he was thrown away. With the exception of the celebration of life for his little cousin who had succumbed to cancer at age 7, he never entered a church again after that fateful encounter within the youth circle.

Ben had studied the Bible more than anyone whom I knew. He found it fascinating, especially when researching historical connotations, and he accepted the message of love. But then, the ugly judgment he received created conflict and frustration. After the final straw of the attack in the youth group circle, he identified himself as agnostic. In pushing him out of the mission trip, he felt the church formed a separation between him and Christ! He felt discarded. I believe that the prolonged conflict without resolution chipped away at his faith in humanity. The conflict destroyed even the last speck of faith. I have always believed, however, that God had not abandoned him.

Eyes were closed, God was misused, and Ben was declared a threat by his church—even as North Carolina debated and voted and passed the short-lived Amendment One.

The voices of layered hate eventually outweighed the voices of love. Layers . . . school trauma by peers and authority, spiritual trauma inflicted by those in authority, laws ranking the human experience debated and passed . . . layer upon layer. Ben died alone. Eyes were not opened. He did not survive. Ben was born in 1991. Ben died in 2013.

One day when eyes have been opened, may society not replace one marginalized group of individuals to be treated cruelly with another group. Will we say again, "How could they have thought such a thing? How was God used in such a disgraceful and life-taking way?"

The fruit of one's actions of his authentic self being incompatible is a bad, bad fruit! Even John Wesley, the founder of Methodism is popularly quoted as providing three simple rules for the church: "First, do no harm; second, do good; and third, stay in love with God." I believe, the church has dressed herself up in sheep's clothing:

> Beware of false prophets, which come to you in sheep's clothing, but inwardly they are ravening wolves." (Matthew 7:15 KJV)

Singing songs of love and praise—unfortunately, in a determination of rightness and dogma—some have identified prey, hunted them down and maimed them, as if consumed by a hungry wolf.

To those Christians who believe their faith justifies and requires judgment, rejection, shaming or abandonment of a fellow human based on sexual orientation, perhaps the following may provide a path to love:

> With what shall I come before the LORD
> and bow down before the exalted God?
> Shall I come before him with burnt offerings,
> with calves a year old?
> Will the LORD be pleased with thousands of rams,
> with ten thousand rivers of olive oil?
> Shall I offer my firstborn for my transgression,
> the fruit of my body for the sin of my soul?
> He has shown you, O mortal, what is good.
> **And what does the LORD require of you?**
> **To act justly and to love mercy**
> **and to walk humbly with your God.**   Micah 6:6-8 RSV

179

***

The suffering brought to Ben by rejection and judgment has been heart shattering for me. I experienced the strength and determination of a mother, yet learned that I could not fully protect or shelter my dear child. Sometimes my best intentions or plans did not prove to be positive for him. I do have peace in knowing that I would have done anything for Ben within my power and that a stronger love does not exist than what I have for him. I know that he knows that.

When the kind officers stood in my family room on May 8, 2013, and after I realized that his death was by suicide, one of the first things I said out loud was, "I'm so glad that he was not a victim of a hate crime." I'm not sure why this is what came to mind, but I think that there was something inside of me that felt some strange sort of relief. While yes, he was a victim, and he must have been depressed, I felt thankful that someone else did not inflict this death upon him. Maybe it is because so much had already been dumped on him. And he soaked it all in.

While I have lost so much, I have also been given exactly what I need to use Ben's life, pain and joy, as an instrument of peace. I have understood from the beginning that it is my purpose to speak Ben's truth . . . to make people see. I have been willing to accept and live with the potential discomfort—fear of judgment regarding the topic of homosexuality and fear of vulnerability in exposing our family's lives. In addition, I have been willing to accept and live with the fear of writing and speaking (both of which terrify me). If some must live with the disapproval of *being* every day, surely I can get comfortable with *some* discomfort. It is about allowing all that should be—God, Ben and probably much more than I can understand—to work through me.

***

In twenty-one years, Ben experienced all of it. He was loved and he loved as much as possible. Ben was rejected, belittled and shamed as much as one could be. He laughed fully and without reserve. Peace, joy, gentleness, kindness became betrayal, aloneness, misunderstanding. Convicted. His Life.

Ben happily in nature with friends.

Photo courtesy of Caitlyn Lineberry.

When standing under the trees, the light came through in the space between that which shaded the light, the leaves. Yet the spring leaves, new and green, vibrated in the frequency of growth and life. Life—a learning field of beauty, joy, peace and heart-wrenching confusion, sadness, loneliness and grief.

***

May each of us commit ourselves to seek out the stones that have been thrown toward us and by us. May we name the stones, struggle and grieve their impact. May we use the newfound understandings to create healing ripples and paths toward reconciliation. May we be kind, thoughtful and humbly see the beauty within all. May we never misuse God. May we omit mindsets of "us and them" and create paradigms of connection, kind regard, healing and love. May we give and accept forgiveness. May we pick up the stones of pain and use them to build an altar to the God of love.

AFTERWORD

Within in a couple of weeks of Ben's death, I was fortunate to receive individual grief counseling and later to participate in a Survivors of Suicide support group at Hospice. The group experience was powerful in understanding and gave me evidence that there is the possibility that this horrific loss may be survived.

In addition, a month after Ben's death, our girls were each scheduled to see a grief counselor for children at Hospice. I explained to the girls what to expect. They did not want to go, but I explained that we must have support to manage our loss in the healthiest way possible. Even though they maintained their opinion, I also stayed firm. I needed to know that others, professionals, were helping my girls through this.

The day arrived, and it was time to leave for the appointment. Sophie bounced through the house, wearing one of Ben's tie-dye tee shirts and carrying a bag of family pictures. She was 10.

Lacy, 12, said, "I'm not going."

I said, "Honey, this is a time that I have to make the decision that I think is in your best interest. We are going to go."

Soon, Lacy entered a full-blown melt down. I approached her to put my arm around her. She screamed, "Don't touch me!" She stayed with me, though. She did not run away. She stayed with me.

In my mind, I was panicked. *Do I force her to go? Do I give in? What is best? What role do I play here?* I thought of Ben who could always soothe her when afraid. He walked many steps with Lacy on his back, and he loved his big brother role. In my mind, I called out, *Help me, Ben.*

Lacy sat in our formal dining room chair with her short little legs dangling. I could picture Ben squatting beside her with his arm around her shoulders and his head against her head. I just imagined it. Soon, Lacy got up and walked to the car.

We checked in at Hospice and sat in the waiting room. Sophie was called back first. She hopped right up and left with the counselor. Lacy and I chit-chatted and looked at a book. Sophie returned and it was time for Lacy. She stood up and walked with the therapist. I felt relief and calm. I was so thankful that she went with the kind lady. Sophie began doing her own thing. I picked up my phone and checked my work email. There was no time-sensitive need for a response. Then I clicked on my personal email.

On the top of the list of emails that included who it was from and in bold, indicating unread letters, was Williambenjaminw. That was Ben's email address. An email from three years earlier had resent to me. The contents were pictures of puppies that we were helping find homes for. Just sweet little puppy faces.

I am humbled and amazed to be the recipient of such a powerful message: "Yes, Mom, I'm here."

***

In June, a month after Ben died, I had the first vivid dream. I was sitting at a small, square table across from Ben. Bill was to my left, in between Ben and myself. It seemed that we may have been outside at a restaurant on a sunny day. Ben was excited to see us and beamed with joy! Although he was 21 when he died, he said, "Here I am, 26. The others are 19, but I am 26!"

I have no idea what he meant, but he was very proud and happy. He looked about the way he did when he was about 14 or 15. He seemed thrilled! I was overwhelmed with joy when I woke up.

***

I had been going to bereavement counseling at Hospice for several months. I had great rapport with the therapist. I really connected with her and could feel her authentic care. My feelings were validated and my self-blaming thoughts were challenged and restated.

Early into one particular session, she asked, "How are you doing?"

I thoughtfully tried to put into words my current state of coping. "I feel like an observer who is looking over everything, as if I'm seeing all that has happened and how it is connected. I feel I am gaining perspective. It is a very interesting phase . . ." My focus turned to the window.

In the small therapy room, the therapist sat in front of the window, and I faced her. Her desk was in the corner to her left and to my right. As I was talking, a magnificent red-tailed hawk swooped in from the right, landing on the window edge, just to the right of her shoulder. Only about eight feet and glass were between me and this beautiful, majestic creature. He was looking toward me with his head making quick, jerky movements. His body and feathers were strong and huge. The primary color was reddish-brown, the feathers scalloped with black and white as if someone had painted with precise care. The coloring around his eyes was an off-white, yet with a line that came out to the side that reminded me of the markings of a chipmunk. The rest of his head was the reddish-brown. I dared not move but whispered, "Turn around very slowly."

The counselor's face looked puzzled as she turned her swivel chair in slow motion toward the right. She turned back to me with her mouth completely open and continued to swivel to face her computer. She keyed to search:

TOTEM ANIMAL HAWK.

She then read,

SYMBOLIZES PERSPECTIVE,
OVERVIEW AND INSIGHT.

We were awestruck by this beautiful gift.

The introduction to the meaning of the hawk offered validation. I was left with pebbles of understanding, comfort and spiritual connection. This experience brought so much more than my human mind was aware of or could understand before.

The hawk stayed with us for several minutes until he flew to a tree farther away and then lifted off again to leave our view.

This gift is acknowledged and received with gratitude.

***

In another dream about a year later, Ben showed me a necklace that he was wearing. He said, "Look, I want you to know about this!"

The necklace had a green, larger, round stone in the middle with small, oval shaped yellow stones making a half arch across the bottom. There was a second row of the yellow stones. He was so excited. My interpretation was that he had healed or accomplished something in some way. He just wanted me to know.

***

In a dream in 2014, to my right was Ben. We were up high and looking out over an amazing scene. There were mountains on either side with a river snaking through the hills. Close to us and down was a bank filled with yellow and pink lilies. The petals were covered in spots. The greens and blues of the sky, mountains and river were breathtakingly vivid and the yellow and pink was stunning. He just wanted me to see.

***

On the year that Ben died, my birthday, his death day, his service and Mother's Day fell within eight days of each other. I know that Ben would not have wanted the timing or any of it to be so hard. One day I learned the typed symbol for a hug: ((( ))). I now have a new perspective regarding the cluster of events. I am hugged up on my birthday, enter into grief and am hugged up again on Mother's Day. Shifts in perception can surely bring comfort.

***

Ben came to me in a dream. He looked as he did just before he died at age 21. I ran to him saying, "You came. You came to see me. You are here." Sobbing, I held him, with my arms up and around his shoulders and he held me. I said, "I know you are dead and I am dreaming, but I feel you with every bit of sensory information that I would if awake and with you alive. I stroked his hair. I noticed that my arms were now around my 3-year-old little Ben as I held him on my lap with his head on my chest. I kissed the top of his light blond hair. I rocked him in the fulfillment of pure love.

My dear, dear son. Thank you for coming to me.

***

In another dream, in the spring of 2019, I watched as Ben, Lacy and Sophie laughed and played. Ben was being silly about his hair standing up like it always looked when he first got up in the mornings. Each child was in complete belly laughs. Each was the same age, which I would guess to be about 4 years old. I was filled with such joy in watching the simple interplay of connection and love. It felt so right. I felt tremendous fulfillment, satisfaction peace, contentment. Bliss.

***

In the spring of 2013, Bill was in a conversation with a dear retired minister, Jack Thomas, who had authored a book, *Traveling to Marshall*. Jack lived in an apartment on the campus where Bill was administrator of the nursing home. Bill told Jack about Ben being in college in Asheville and his dream of being a writer. Jack shared that he had worked with a publishing company in Asheville, Grateful Steps. He offered, "Let me see if they need an intern." Jack had it all worked out! Ben had a connection. My very last communication with Ben was my leaving a message about this arrangement. Ben died that week. Jack let the Executive Director, Micki Cabaniss, know.

Since Ben's death, I have felt responsible to share his story by writing a book to help others who are being victimized. But I felt inadequate, unskilled and overwhelmed. I just couldn't seem to move forward in making it happen. I just could not do it. I received regular supportive encouragement from Jack and others. The family had planned to visit Asheville on May 8, 2019, to complete some maintenance around his memorial tree on campus. A few weeks before, it dawned on me that maybe I could reach out to Grateful Steps to request a meeting. Micki, the executive director, met with me, a few miles from where Ben died, and on an anniversary of Ben's death day. We got to know each other in the office where Ben was going to be an intern. From then on, this book has been written with ease and with tremendous support. Micki has challenged me, taught me and used her gifts to nurture this process.

UNCA memorial tree.
Be Kind – Be Creative – Be You.

ACKNOWLEDGMENTS

Thank you:

—to the God of love who reassures me regularly that whether here in earth school or there in the life after, we are being held in constant connection.

—to family and friends for your support and Susan and friends for sharing your photography. Bill, we have created a life that has been full of mutual respect and care, beauty and pain—always with deep meaning.

—to our dear children . . . all we could have ever wished for.

—to Green Street UMC and Pastor Kelly, for being "the real deal"; to Bishop Melvin Talbert, for being a gentle and fierce advocate and role model; and to agencies such as Reconciling Ministries Network, Believe Out Loud, The Trevor Project, and the Tyler Clementi Foundations, for being a voice for many.

—to Jack Thomas, for showing me a path for sharing Ben's story.

—to my publisher, Micki Cabaniss, and to my copy editor, Cathy Mitchell.